Northern Scotland

VOLUME 2 2011

Edited by Marjory Harper and David Worthington

Edinburgh University Press

Subscription rates for 2011

One volume per year, published in May

		UK	Rest of World	N. America
Institutions	Print	£42.00	£45.00	$82.00
	Online	£37.00	£37.00	$68.00
	Print and online	£52.00	£56.00	$102.00
	Back issues/ single copies	£42.00	£45.00	$82.00
Individuals	Print	£23.00	£26.00	$48.00
	Online	£23.00	£23.00	$42.00
	Print and online	£29.00	£32.50	$60.00
	Back issues/ single copies	£23.00	£26.00	$48.00

Postage

Print only and print plus online prices include packaging and airmail for subscribers in North America. Print only and print plus online subscriptions for subscribers in the Rest of the world include packaging and surface mail postage. Please add a further £6 if you would like your subscription posted by airmail.

Payment options

All orders must be accompanied by the correct payment. You can pay by cheque in Pounds Sterling or US Dollars, bank transfer, Direct Debit or Credit/Debit Card. The individual rate applies only when a subscription is paid for with a personal cheque, credit card or bank transfer from a personal account.

To order using the online subscription form, please visit www.eupjournals.com/nor/page/subscribe

To place your order by credit card, phone +44 (0)131 650 6207, fax on +44 (0)131 662 3286 or email journals@eup.ed.ac.uk. Don't forget to include the expiry date of your card, the security number (three digits on the reverse of the card) and the address that the card is registered to.

Cheques must be made payable to Edinburgh University Press Ltd. Sterling cheques must be drawn on a UK bank account.

If you would like to pay by bank transfer or Direct Debit, contact us at journals@eup.ed.ac.uk and we will provide instructions.

Advertising

Advertisements are welcomed and rates are available on request, or by consulting our website at www.eupjournals.com. Advertisers should send their enquiries to the Journals Marketing Manager at the address above.

CONTENTS

CONTRIBUTORS v

ARTICLES

Victoria Henshaw, A Reassessment of the British Army in Scotland, from the Union to the '45   1

Alistair Mutch, A Contested Eighteenth-Century Election: Banffshire, 1795   22

Suzanne Rigg, Scots in the Hudson's Bay Company, c. 1779–c. 1821   36

Eric Richards, Highland Emigration in the Age of Malthus: Scourie, 1841–55   60

Terry Brotherstone, 'I thought I was back in Africa ... and decided to come.' An interview with Professor John D. Hargreaves, Head of History at the University of Aberdeen, 1962–70   83

CORRESPONDENCE

Pomegranates, Opium and Poppycock
Adrian Clark   107

Rejoinder to Professor Cairns Craig
Stuart Wallace   108

REVIEWS

Cynthia J. Neville, *Land, Law and People in Medieval Scotland*
Iain MacInnes   110

Terryl N. Kinder (ed.), *Life on the Edge: The Cistercian Abbey of Balmerino, Fife*
Helen Birkett   112

Margaret Connell Szasz, *Scottish Highlanders and Native Americans: Indigenous Education in the Eighteenth-Century Atlantic World*
James Hunter   115

Colin G. Calloway, *White People, Indians and Highlanders: Tribal Peoples and Colonial Encounters in Scotland and America*
James Hunter   115

Annie Tindley, *The Sutherland Estate, 1850–1920*
Marjory Harper   117

Iain Hutchison, *A History of Disability in Nineteenth-Century Scotland*
John Swinton   121

Catriona M. M. MacDonald, *Whaur Extremes Meet: Scotland's Twentieth Century*
S. Karly Kehoe   123

A full index to the first series of *Northern Scotland* can be found at www.euppublishing.com/journal/nor

CONTRIBUTORS

Terry Brotherstone is senior lecturer (retired) and director of the 'Lives in the Oil Industry' oral history project, University of Aberdeen.

Victoria Henshaw is a doctoral student at the University of Birmingham.

Alistair Mutch is Professor of Information and Learning, Nottingham Trent University.

Eric Richards is Professor of History, Flinders University, Adelaide, South Australia.

Suzanne Rigg is Museum Supervisor, Biggar Museum Trust.

A REASSESSMENT OF THE BRITISH ARMY IN SCOTLAND, FROM THE UNION TO THE '45

VICTORIA HENSHAW

The role and reputation of the British army in Scotland in the first half of the eighteenth century is often regarded negatively. The military focus of the Jacobites on Scotland created a need for the army to act as a police force and as the suppressor of political and military dissent. This and the later reinvention of the Jacobites in popular culture, has combined to create a series of half-truths and prejudices against the government army in Scotland. It is remembered as an army of occupation from England, which acted brutally, with legal impunity or worse, the tacit or outright consent of its commanding officers. Meanwhile, the Jacobite army's endorsement of the wearing of tartan as a unifier during the '45, regardless of origin, allows the continuing misconception that the Jacobite army was Scottish, and specifically Highland, in make up.[1] The Scottish National Party's desire to encourage a sense of 'Scottishness' in order to achieve eventual independence has directed focus on the last attempt to reverse the Union: the Jacobite rebellions. Though several legal and political disputes were closer to achieving this, military rebellions provide a more enduring defiance.[2] This has affected the angle of recent historiography that centres on the Jacobite army and its Scottish elements to the detriment of the government army.

There are many reasons for the negative view of the British army between the Union and Culloden. The perception of the British army's unqualified success from the Revolutionary wars onwards forces an erroneous connection between the British army of the eighteenth century and the armies of a lawless earlier era. The reputation of the British army in Scotland is thus coloured by the events of the War of the Three Kingdoms, the actions of the Protectorate's army and the turbulent religious conflict of the seventeenth century that continued in Scotland after the Restoration. The drowning of Margaret Wilson and Margaret Maclauchlan on 11 May 1685[3] and the use of the Highland Host to subdue religious dissent in 1678 created a cultural memory of brutality and the army's involvement in it. One diarist, after his participation in the Battle of Bothwell Bridge in June 1679, recorded the army's behaviour: 'The ruffians [government soldiers] fell to their work, beating and bruising the servants, because they would not tell them where I was.'[4] This is despite the absence of recorded killings by the Host[5] and evidence that Presbyterian martyr mythology is guilty of perpetuating legend at the expense of truth.[6] The Protectorate's army, the Host and the military suppression of religious dissent combined to create a popular memory of the army as an oppressive police force. It is true that the garrison records of 1656 include fourteen regiments in Scotland[7] and this represented a relatively high number of troops. However, few, such as the garrison at Finlarig by Loch Tay, were positioned to subdue.[8] Most were located in the Borders and Lowlands or along the coast against possible invasions.[9] This association with the previous century over-rode the military advances of the period. The perception of an army of poorly trained soldiers or mercenaries, recruited from the scum of the earth, belies the changes made by improved technology, tactics and the development of a fiscal-military state, which was able to support larger armies that allowed improved training. This increased discipline.[10] The remainder of this paper will seek to re-examine the role and reputation of the British army in Scotland and establish the extent of such perceptions.

The greatest misapprehension is in regard to the army's role, size and dominance in Scotland. The replacement of Tory 'blue water policy' with Whig-favoured land-based warfare, which required a large and expensive permanent army, emphasised by memories of military enforcement of government policy in the seventeenth century, combined to create a fear of standing armies in both public and political circles.[11] Consequently, Britain had a considerably smaller army than its continental counterparts at least until 1763. Half of this was deployed to Ireland, while only one quarter was allocated to serve within Britain, encompassing both England and Scotland.[12] Additionally, the usual practice of running regiments under strength led the duke of Richmond to doubt their ability to defend Scotland at the outbreak of the '45.[13] Indeed, at Prestonpans, the first battle of the rebellion, the government force of 2,400 was outnumbered by the Jacobites, at 2,500, who had yet to gather their maximum strength.[14] Even by Culloden, most British army regiments were functioning on an average of 427 men of their 500 total strength.[15] A series of letters, two months before the start of the '15, between Sir Robert Pollock (Governor of Fort William) and James Graham, 1st duke of Montrose (Secretary of State for Scotland) reveals the handicap of under-strength regiments on garrisoning abilities. On 7 June 1715, Pollock reported his concern that the plan to remove one of the two regiments at Fort William would make keeping outposts untenable, especially as they were already functioning under strength due to disease and desertion.[16] Pollock included a return that listed the two regiments, Hill's and Hamilton's, at a paper strength of 425 men. However, of these eighty-seven privates were stationed at four outposts, forty-eight were off sick, forty-one had deserted and 161 had died since the last return. This left an effective force of eighty-eight men to defend Fort William and run patrols or operations against Jacobites in the area.[17]

Additionally, those stationed in Scotland suffered from poor training and outdated tactics; garrison troops were of lesser priority than elite regiments engaged on the continent in 'legitimate' warfare. The garrison troops, who made up a significant proportion, if not the total of the government's immediate reaction force in Scotland during rebellions, rarely fired more than a few volleys during training.[18] Their role in garrisons was as a police force and on anti-smuggling patrols.[19] This meant they rarely formed up as full regiments to train en masse as they would if fighting a set-piece battle.[20] By contrast, Cumberland's army prior to Culloden had six weeks of dedicated drill practice to prepare.[21] Moreover, what basic training garrison troops received was for conventional continental-style combat, not the unexpected tactic of the Highland Charge.[22] This was especially true at Prestonpans and still a factor at Falkirk. By Culloden, the element of surprise was gone and the government troops were prepared for it, contributing greatly to their success.

The British fear of standing armies also put the British army at an administrative disadvantage. In practice this meant a reliance on the Secretaries of State for Scotland and their deputies as the government's representatives in Scotland. This included both formal and informal positions. The latter were dominated by the 2nd and 3rd dukes of Argyll, and their clients, Duncan Forbes of Culloden (the Lord President) and Lord Milton (the Lord Justice Clerk) – consequently known as the 'Argathelians'. Beneath them, the army relied on a range of civic posts: four Lord Provosts, Lords Lieutenant and their deputies, magistrates, constables and postmasters.[23] The handicap of a civil-led army is demonstrated through intelligence gathering. The news that Charles Edward had landed on 25 July 1745 was passed from a parishioner in Ardnamurchan to her minister on 4 August. He, via the local Bailie, informed the Sheriff of Argyllshire who notified the duke of Argyll.[24] It was only at this point that the news reached military hands, as Lord Milton, the Lord Justice Clerk, was fortuitously at Argyll's home when the intelligence arrived. Milton then informed Sir John Cope, Commander-in-Chief of the Forces in Scotland on 8 August.[25] By contrast, Fort William, twenty-five miles from the landing site, learnt of the landing a day later than Cope, in Edinburgh, despite the presence of a recruiting officer at the Baillie's house on 4 August. Fort William's letter informing the General did not arrive until 13 August.[26] This reveals the relative capability of civil and military communication channels, the difference in importance of landowners and officers, and an army which lacked a dominant intelligence-gathering and communication procedure.[27] What is key is that, even in 1745, the army was not the insuperable machine popularly imagined.

Significantly, official espionage was also politically focused,[28] something which left the army in the field reliant on ad hoc spies or information gained by locals.[29] This was not always a successful tactic; when facing a Jacobite invasion as far south as Derby in December 1745, the British army was dependent on the possibly unreliable information of a largely unknown volunteer spy, called Dudley

Bradstreet.³⁰ Interestingly, though he received his last instructions from the duke of Cumberland, the new Commander-in-Chief, before joining the Jacobite camp, Bradstreet was initially commissioned by the duke of Newcastle, Secretary of State for the Southern Department – a civilian.³¹ Such use of civilians was less a failing of the British army, than of contemporary practices. The Jacobite army did the same, relying on the local knowledge of the earl of Kilmarnock at Falkirk and that of local man, Robert Anderson, to reposition the army before Prestonpans.³²

Another aspect in which the British army in Scotland has been misrepresented, is in the physical infrastructure of occupation. In many ways, barracks, forts and roads are symbols of occupation, especially given the late seventeenth- and early eighteenth-century attitude towards the standing army.³³ Their location was consciously chosen to have strategic significance, to shorten marching time, and to guard road links. They also provided a presence in disaffected areas, such as the barracks of Inversnaid on Rob 'Roy' MacGregor's confiscated land.³⁴ However, beyond their existence, they were hardly domineering. The correspondence between Pollock, Fort William's governor, and Montrose, the Secretary of State for Scotland, suggests an isolated and physically vulnerable fort rather than a base of oppression. Nearly two months into the '15, Pollock wrote that he doubted Fort William's ability to survive a siege. The outposts' lack of independent water supply left them dependent on the main fort and they were therefore 'useless' and too far from the Fort to allow for good communications. Fort William itself had no drawbridge and its parapets were incomplete, forcing Pollock to order logs be used to complete them.³⁵ A month later he reported that Cameron of Lochiel, a prominent Jacobite chief, had marched 500 men within two miles of the Fort. He added

> yr Grace may easily Judge how mortifying it was to me to have those ungreate & unnatural rebells pass under my Nose, without giving them the least disturbance, nor am I in the least condition to offend their Country in their absence, my Number not being sufficient [eighty-eight at the return two months previously.] [I] dare not leave a place of this Consequence.³⁶

When a true test of the fortifications occurred during the '45, Fort George, Fort Augustus and Ruthven fell to the Jacobites.³⁷ Fort William was besieged for a fortnight, in March and April 1746, but did not fall, saved by fortuitous timing and superior siting to Fort Augustus.³⁸

Another view of barracks is as an advancement. While France had 160 barracks by 1710, Britain continued to scatter its soldiers across the country in billets, to the detriment of discipline and response time.³⁹ The legacy of military oppression during the War of the Three Kingdoms and the 'No Standing Army' debate meant billeting on civilians was forbidden in the Disbanding Act of 1679 and Mutiny Act of 1689.⁴⁰ Interestingly for Scotland, however, it appears that a difference in law meant private billeting in Scotland could still happen,⁴¹ though only larger landowners endured 'roistering', either to demonstrate their loyalty or as a punishment for disaffection.[42] Rather than objects of oppression, the decision to build barracks was seen as a way to save the population from the burden of billeting, and, by keeping soldiers together, discipline and control over soldiers was increased.[43] Barracks, therefore, were representative of the change in government attitude to soldiers, both financially and with regard to the old fear of standing armies. Scotland's position as a border area, with a potentially volatile population and vast coastline, susceptible to invasion, presented an opportunity where barracks could be developed and perfected. The rate of improvement is shown by their development from the soldier-built fortified barracks c. 1717 which borrowed much architecturally from the tower houses of seventeenth-century chieftains, to the construction of a complete Vauban-inspired fortress at Ardersier outside Inverness c. 1748–69. This development demonstrates the increasing level of investment and interest the government took in the accommodation of its soldiers.[44]

The dramatic increase in roads built by and for the military from 1725 was intended to aid the response of the British army to potential invasions and rebellions. However, they were not unwanted by many Scots. Even after the '45, the earl of Rothes requested that a sergeant and twelve men be sent to instruct his men in road construction in 1749. Though his request was denied because no men could be spared from building the roads in the Highlands,[45] his example shows both that landowners wanted roads and that the government's priority was focused on those roads that had military significance. Additionally, because the upkeep of the roads and bridges was organised and administered by the Scottish elite at a local government level (and by the Commissioners of Supply as the eighteenth century progressed[46]), they were not solely a policy imposed by an oppressive London-based government but had local support amongst Scottish political and social elites.

One of the biggest myths concerning the British army's behaviour in Scotland between the Union and Culloden was its place outside the law. In reality, the authority of the military was strictly limited, something best demonstrated by the army's involvement in riot suppression. The Riot Act of 1715 converted rioting from a misdemeanour under common law, to a felony. Consequently, both private individuals and the authorities could respond with force and were immune from punishment for injuring or killing rioters. From 1715 onwards the mob had one hour to disperse once the Riot Act had been read to them, at which point magistrates could call in the army or militia to scatter them by force.[47] The transfer of power to the magistrate made military intervention a civilian not a martial decision. This frequently hampered the army's response or allowed for confused command structures that permitted mistakes to occur. Specifically, there was a fundamental misunderstanding regarding when military force could be introduced. Was it when violence was first used by the mob or only after the hour had passed since the reading of the Act? Guides published for the magistrates who would face these questions were vague and impractical.

Even MPs lacked understanding that authorities could still intervene before, as well as after, the hour given in the Riot Act using common law if the rioters used violence.[48]

Ironically, the failure of the civil administration to understand and use the Act successfully, effectively tied the hands of the army. The magistrates' caution at using the army during the 1725 Malt Tax riots in Glasgow meant that the rioters were able to take control of the town.[49] Militarily, the same confusion meant that at the outbreak of the '45 no-one in Scotland believed they held the authority to raise militias or loyal clans, despite many requests to do so.[50] This hesitation over authority led to the fall of Edinburgh to the Jacobites, and its Provost, Archibald Stewart, to a trial for neglect of duty. Though he was found not guilty, the fact that he was tried at all shows he was right to question his authority and the support of the government.[51] Even in 1759, with a rumoured invasion of 20,000 French troops on the Clyde, calls to raise the militia could not be acted upon because of confusion regarding authority.[52]

The soldiers of the British army were also governed by the rules stipulated in the Mutiny Act of 1689. This was introduced after the slow show of support by the army at the Glorious Revolution, and brought actions such as desertion, previously tried under civil law as a felony, into the Articles of War, which allowed harsher punishments. Additionally, it also gave the army power to maintain control and discipline over its soldiers.[53]

The combination of the Riot Act and the Mutiny Act meant that soldiers were not above the law. Sergeant Davies, for example, was found guilty of murder and hanged for killing Robert Park in 1712 when the Riot Act had not been read.[54] In 1737, Corporal Lang and Private McAdams were tried for the murder of suspected smuggler Hugh Fraser on 4 June 1735. Both were found guilty and hanged as their warrant had been issued by their commanding officer, not a magistrate, and their authority was ruled invalid. The authorities' worry concerning their legitimacy, together with the introduction, and use, of laws that limited the power of the army, demonstrates that the institution of law was stronger than the army and that the military were not uncontrolled or legally immune.[55]

That is not to say that the army was a-political. There was, in fact, much cross-over between military and civil authority, which was inevitable considering the nature of a gentry-led society. Army officers were often MPs and JPs, and therefore influenced local law keeping too.[56] Simon Fraser, 11th Lord Lovat, was simultaneously commander of an Independent Company and Sheriff of Inverness-shire in the 1730s[57] and Lieutenant-Colonel Blackader was Deputy Governor of Stirling Castle and the local JP between 1719 and 1728.[58] The army was also vulnerable to a magistrate's abuse of power. The superiority of magistrates over officers that had been established by the Riot Act meant that if a magistrate was invested in the outcome of elections or was a client of the local MPs (who were often from the local elite) they could call out the army on voters during elections. During the 1722 elections at Cupar in Fife, a mob protesting the continued dominance of the Leslie family was dispersed by the army. This was influenced by, or on the pretext, that the mob was Jacobite and was acting against the Whig interest represented by the Leslies.[59] Additionally, the physical presence of a garrison could be used to intimidate, and the government consciously did so with the four fortified barracks commissioned in 1717. Bernera at Glenelg, for example, was sited on Macleod land and overlooked the area controlled by the chief of the Mackenzies, William Mackenzie, 5th earl of Seaforth. He was Catholic and had brought his clan out for the Jacobites in the '15 and '19.[60]

Another key politicisation of the army was the government's use of commissions and promotions of officers to influence the socio-political makeup of the army. Military service provided an avenue for the political elite to discover those who could help further their aims. This often had a direct impact on who was put in positions of power in the army, politics and diplomacy. The duke of Marlborough was well-known for this, using his heightened powers as Captain-General during the War of the Spanish Succession to the benefit of the 2nd earl of Stair and the 2nd duke of Argyll, who both gained military promotion, diplomatic and political appointments.[61] Many worried that the longer the war continued, the greater the number of new Whig MPs there would be in the Commons acting as Marlborough's 'placemen'.[62]

One benefit of issuing commissions strategically was their use as bribes or rewards for loyalty, thus affecting both the political leanings of the army and the society from which its men were drawn. On 13 September 1745, at the outbreak of the '45 rebellion, eighteen commissions for Independent Highland Companies were issued to be distributed by Duncan Forbes of Culloden (the Lord President) to loyal or unsure chiefs. In return they would be expected to raise their clan for the government instead of against it.[63] This strategy met with some success. The duke of Sutherland received commissions for two companies in recognition of his past loyalty.[64] He and his clan had fought for the government during the '15 and '19.[65] His involvement ensured the capture of the earl of Cromartie and his son on 15 April 1746, which deprived the Jacobite army of 300–400 men the day before Culloden.[66]

However, the strategy also backfired. Those not favoured were quick to take offence or were provided with the ideal excuse to join the Jacobites. The Grant clan had a history of loyal service for the government going back to the Independent Companies raised in 1701 and the 800 men provided to assist in the liberation of Inverness during the '15.[67] However, Sir James Grant of Grant was insulted by the offer of only one Company at the outbreak of the '45, when others, such as the MacLeods of Skye and Harris, were offered four.[68] This, and the years of financial loss acting as army, police and election managers for the government without recompense, meant Grant did only the bare minimum required to remain loyal during the '45. Though he stopped Grant septs being recruited by the Jacobites, he made no attempt to stop or intercept

Jacobite movements. Indeed, some consciousness of the fine line he walked is demonstrated in the records he kept to prove his loyalty. These were indeed investigated after the rebellion.[69]

Perhaps the most well-known failure of the policy to ensure loyalty in exchange for commissions was Simon Fraser, 11th Lord Lovat. Lovat is often portrayed as a self-serving man with no motivation but the expansion of his power base. However, this belies the importance to chiefs of maintaining power over their clan: Lovat himself spent a life-time ensuring the security of his title and estates. As power came through patronage – both that which he received and that which he was consequently able to distribute – Lovat needed demonstrations of patronage, such as political posts or army commissions. These displayed his power to his clan who might otherwise have begun to look for support elsewhere.[70] The award of one of the six Independent Companies raised in the aftermath of General Wade's report into the state of Scotland's defences in 1725, which Lovat kept for fourteen years, fulfilled this need. However, the loss of a captaincy in an Independent Company in April 1717 after only eight months, the Governorship of Inverness in 1718 after only one year, a state pension in 1727 and a Sheriffship in 1739[71] were significant factors in Lovat's lack of belief in the government's favour when the '45 began. This, combined with the government's lethargy in issuing commissions, meant Lovat felt no incentive to remain loyal and joined the Jacobites.[72] The problem was that while Lovat's past disloyalty might not have deserved rewards, the Fraser clan's considerable numbers and its importance in the region affected the decisions of others: Lovat 'was instrumental in getting the weak and inept earl of Cromartie to rise [in 1745].'[73]

Though the issue of commissions illustrates the government's understanding of the power of patronage, it suffered from limited success because the government in London was slow to react to the '45 rebellion. In early September 1745 '[The Secretary of State for Scotland] Tweeddale still did not believe the news that Prince Charles Edward had landed in Scotland ... the Under-Secretary of State, Andrew Mitchell, was even more sceptical.'[74] Forbes was left, therefore, to use his personal network of acquaintances to persuade Scotland's elite to remain neutral, if not loyal, on the promise of commissions. For many, such as Kenneth Mackenzie, Lord Fortrose, Sir Alexander Macdonald of Sleat and Norman Macleod of Skye, such promises were enough, especially as the growing government force gathered at Inverness.[75] However, when the commissions did not arrive until 10 October, nineteen days after the Jacobite victory at Prestonpans, it was too late for the more impatient chiefs like Lovat and Cromartie.[76] Even if they used the lack of commissions as an excuse for joining the rising, the plausibility of the excuse shows that such an insult would have been considered important to contemporaries.

Another myth regarding the British army in Scotland concerns the perception that the Government and the Jacobite supporters were split along lines of nationality. This belies a more complex movement with international ties and ignores other motivations than simple nationality. In reality, decisions of loyalty were more often made on issues of religion. The seventeenth-century struggle for dominance as Church of Scotland between the Episcopal and Presbyterian churches continued into the eighteenth century with the preservation of a separate Church of Scotland in the Union treaty. The strongly-held principles behind religious beliefs meant that the Oath of Allegiance (1689) and the Oath of Abjuration (1701), both of which recognised the protestant succession, were unacceptable to many Scottish Episcopalians and English non-jurors.[77] Their readiness to lose power, position and income through the forfeiture of their offices underlined the potency of religion as a driver of identity and allegiance. Religion also impacted upon the political world in another sense, as the strongly patriarchal precepts of the Old Testament coloured questions of political legitimacy.[78] Religious and political principles were therefore closely intertwined and equally uncompromising. Such differences could split communities and families, creating a civil war facet to the period of Jacobite activity.

The Murrays of Atholl were an excellent example of the effects of this. At first glance, they appear as the archetypal family who, strategically, had sons on both sides of the Jacobite-Government divide. Of the men of adult age from Glorious Revolution to Culloden, seven served the government, either as loyal peers or in the army and navy, while seven supported the Jacobites, both politically and militarily. Significantly, the political split is mirrored identically by a difference in religion: those who supported the government were Presbyterian, while those who joined the Jacobites became Episcopalian. The most famous of the family were William, Jacobite duke of Atholl or Marquess of Tullibardine to the Hanoverians, and his General brother, Lord George Murray. Their correspondence shows the depth of their loyalty to 'the Cause'. In March 1746 George began a siege of the family seat, Blair Castle, writing to William: 'Dear Brother... Our duty here is constant and fatiguing; but we grudge nothing that is for His Royal Highness's service and the good of the Cause... If we get the Castle I hope you will excuse our demolishing it.' William replied: 'Our great-great-grandfather, grandfather, and father's pictures will be an irreparable loss on blowing up the house. But there is no comparison to be made with these faint images of our fore-fathers and the more necessary public service which requires we should sacrifice everything.'[79] Similarly, the 4th earl of Kilmarnock is usually dismissed as motivated entirely by debt in his decision to join the Jacobites.[80] However, private letters between him and his wife reveal a deep religious belief that would have made service against the Jacobites difficult. 'God, who orders every thing as it ought to be, must be trusted in, and he will bring everything about for the best. Let us pray to him, thank him, and resign our Selves to his Will.'[81]

The multiple facets to loyalty meant that service in the British army was actively sought by Scots in as many numbers as those that supported the Jacobites. Since the Glorious Revolution forced the decision of allegiance and the Union created one country, the pro-protestant succession element of the Scottish gentry had sought to participate in the elite of Great Britain. The Union treaty preserved a specifically Scottish law, church and education but moved the parliament to Whitehall. The gentry therefore needed to carve out a path into the social and governing elite of London. However, opportunities in politics and the church were much scarcer than in the army with only twenty-four posts allocated to Scottish MPs and sixteen as Representative Peers. From that small pool, those with real power were drawn who decided policy in the 'inner cabinate' as advisors to the crown. This did not include a Scottish politician or advisor until the late eighteenth century.[82] Military service, however, suited the martial spirit of the Scottish gentry and provided an education and occupation compatible with gentry status – in 1748, Loudoun's Highland Regiment included thirty-eight servants and batmen for officers.[83] During the seventeenth century, Scots served in French, Swedish, Russian and the Dutch forces, and as the British army expanded over the eighteenth century, more were able to serve in British regiments.[84]

The British army, in many ways, began before the creation of Great Britain. Since the Union of Crowns in 1603, the army of Scotland joined that of England and Ireland, under the control of one monarch. One legacy of the War of the Three Kingdoms was that on the Restoration in 1660, an effective standing army existed for the first time.[85] Therefore, since the Restoration, Scottish regiments had been working together with English and Irish regiments, both in foreign and domestic deployments.[86] Consequently, Scots, as well as English and Irish soldiers, often formed part of the garrisons in Scotland during both peace and rebellions. The garrison at Inverness in the years straddling the Glorious Revolution, for example, contained Mackenzie's Company, then Grant's Company, until it, along with Kenmuir's and Glencairn's Company, were merged to form Hill's Regiment in 1690. This regiment then garrisoned Inverlochy, and later, Fort William.[87] In 1729, Fort Augustus's garrison included two companies of the 43rd Highland Regiment (later the Black Watch)[88], while at the start of the '45, Gardiner's and Hamilton's Dragoons were made up mainly from Irish recruitment.[89]

There was also a greater mixture of nationalities present at battles during the Jacobite wars than is commonly perceived. At the battles of Killiecrankie (27 July 1689), Dunkeld (21 August 1689) and Cromdale (1 May 1690) opposing forces consisted of Scottish Jacobites and government forces made up of Scottish soldiers who were garrisoning Scotland.[90] Scottish regiments were also present on both sides at Prestonpans, Falkirk and Culloden. At Culloden, four of the sixteen regiments of the line with the British army were Scottish: The Royal Scots (1st of Foot), The Scots Fusiliers, Semphill's and Pulteney's Regiment of Foot. They were supported by two companies of Loudoun's Highlanders, two companies of the 43rd Highland Regiment (later the Black Watch) and three companies of the Argyllshire Militia.[91] The presence of Scottish militia during '15 and '45 also shows that many Scots made a conscious decision to fight against their countrymen for a government and succession they believed in. The Glasgow militia formed part of the defence of Stirling from September to November 1715, while about 300 men from clan Campbell defended Perth in February 1716.[92] Estimates of the total number of Scots in militia service during the '15 vary, from 2–3,000 to 11,000 men.[93] Glasgow also raised 600 men to defend the town and 600 to guard Stirling during the '45, and took part in the fighting at Falkirk.[94] Similarly, when the Edinburgh volunteers were disbanded, many joined the government forces at Prestonpans in September 1745.[95] The focus of local militias on the south-west and west of Scotland during the '45, including Edinburgh, Linlithgow, Perth, Glasgow, Paisley, Kilmarnock, Stirling and Renfrew, highlights the importance of Presbyterian and Whig allegiances in the area.[96]

Despite opposition to the Union and protestant succession, which was something evident in the frequent Jacobite rebellions, many Scots sought and found successful careers within the British state, in its army. From the Restoration onwards over the eighteenth century, the proportion of Scots in the British army increased at a higher percentage than other British nationals. Colonelcies given to Scots increased from a handful under Charles II and three of a potential twenty-six under James II, to 10 per cent of colonelcies at the Union. At Blenheim in 1704, of the sixteen colonelcies, five were Scottish, with seven English and four Irish. By Malplaquet five years later, ten of the twenty-five general officers serving Marlborough were Scottish. Between 1714 and 1756, 20 per cent of colonelcies in the British army were Scottish, despite this being the longest period of peace in the eighteenth century, excepting the eight years of the War of the Austrian Succession.[97] Promotion was also steady: between 1714 and 1763, seventy-eight of 374 new appointments were given to Scots, making Scots 20 per cent of new appointments between 1715 and 1739, and 23 per cent between 1739 and 1763.[98] This 'preferment' of Scots led a contemporary to complain '... had I been a Scott instead of a Cumbrian I should have had a Company long agoe.'[99] In the second half of the century, Scots were actively sought as soldiers and between 1759 and 1793 twenty foot regiments were recruited from the Highlands. From a total population of 300,000, 74,000 fought against France on the continent and in North America,[100] a very high proportion, especially given the decreasing population of Scotland, from a quarter of a million in 1755 to 350,000 in 1830.[101]

Just as the mixed nationality and disproportionately high Scottish element in the British army prevents a conclusion that the army was an English army of occupation, so the accusation of the army's oppressive behaviour in Scotland is overstated. The confusion stems from a mixture of exaggerated genuine events and the perpetuation of myths to support a preconceived agenda. The eight or nine deaths amongst the crowd at the hanging of popular smuggler, Andrew Wilson, which led to the Porteous Riot on 13 April 1736, are true and tragic, but to use this to label all the army's work in Scotland as oppressive is to oversimplify its role.[102] However works, such as Wodrow's *Sufferings,* consciously record only negative events to ensure a rival group's reputation is tarnished, perpetuating the myth of the army's involvement in religious violence by ignoring inconvenient evidence. For example, in a 1684 incident of soldiers who fired on a crowd demanding the release of the prisoners they were escorting, Wodrow writes that the soldiers fired first, when official accounts record that the soldiers were ambushed and then returned fire.[103] Additionally, many of the stories of brutal behaviour occurred during rebellions. It is often forgotten or not understood that according to contemporary law, rooted in the works of Thomas Aquinas and St Augustine, rebels forfeited their rights by rebelling against their 'natural' leader, and so could legally be treated more harshly than civilians or prisoners of war.[104] Though the duke of Cumberland actively attempted to keep his soldiers in check, 'when the line between combatant and civilian was blurred... war could be "total" for those involved.'[105]

A relatively small proportion of soldiers' time was spent against rebels. Instead the main role of the British army was as a police force, to prevent or put down riots and to prevent or capture smugglers.[106] The garrison placement of 1656 shows that the majority of men were positioned along the coastline to act as the third line of defence against smugglers, and as an anti-invasion force.[107] The regular army was also supported by auxiliary troops made up of loyal clans who were formed into Independent Companies. Since the Union of Crowns, Independent Companies had been used sporadically to police troublesome areas. In 1687 for example, the Mackenzie Company was sent against MacDonald of Keppoch for raiding the Laird of Macintosh's lands.[108] The Grants were also used as one of the two Companies raised in 1701 after the difficult years of bad harvests in the 1690s had led to increased robbery and cattle reiving.[109] In later years, when these Independent Companies had been regimented into the 43rd Highland Regiment (later the Black Watch), companies were used to help search and confiscate arms following the Disarming Acts of 1716, 1725 and 1746.[110]

The power and dominance of the British army in the first half of the eighteenth century is also distorted by its eventual success over the Jacobites. While victory seems inevitable with hindsight, the dominance of the government forces at Culloden had to be learned from bitter mistakes during the '45. The shock of defeat at Prestonpans inspired General Hawley to develop a new firing order for Falkirk. When this too failed, Cumberland introduced a new bayonet drill, though, as Duffy argues, this change probably brought success by increasing morale, rather than through practical implementation.[111] Another development that gave the government forces eventual victory was the change in marching column formations. At the start of the '45, the army was using the formation set out by Major General Humphrey Bland in his *Treatise of Military Discipline*.[112] This specified that a platoon marched at ten files wide or a division at twenty-four files wide, as against the Jacobite formation of only three files wide. Cumberland recognised this gave them superior manoeuvrability in the mountains and by April 1746, the British army was so efficient at marching that it was able to form up to engage the enemy twice on the march to Drummossie Muir.[113] Lastly, a major difference leading to success or failure was the quality and experience of the government troops. Those who fought at Prestonpans were essentially garrison troops, while those at Culloden were blooded by the experience of fighting on the continent.[114]

A final important feature that refutes the idea that the British army was a domineering presence in Scotland was the hampering effect of government rather than a lenient, relaxed attitude that tolerated independent authoritarian action. Scotland's distance from London, and the dominance of England in the Union, made Scotland the poor cousin. Its economic dependence, unprotected coastline open to invasion and ungovernable Highlands complete with a pool of militarily capable clansmen ready for rebel recruitment, created an attitude in London that Scotland was a problem. Consequently it only came to government attention at times of trouble, fostering a reactionary rather than preventative attitude to governance.[115] This was especially true concerning the army because of its role as the main line of defence against the above threats. Though nominally in charge, the Secretary of State for Scotland or the Lord Treasurer usually left responsibility for the routine work to three or four clerks supervised by the Under-Secretary of State and to twelve clerks under the supervision of two Treasury secretaries. None had particular understanding of Scotland or Scottish issues[116] and most saw the position as a sinecure not as part of a career.[117] This often led to inconsistent policy that handicapped rather than indulged the army. Just a year after the '15, the Treasury's desire to save money led to the reduction in cannon at Berwick (from seventy-six to fifty), Edinburgh (from fifty to forty), Fort William (from sixty-eight to thirty) and Stirling (which lost two).[118] However, it was the near success of the '15 that triggered the Board of Ordnance to commission four fortified barracks at Ruthven in Badenoch, Kiliwhimen, Inversnaid and Bernera in Glenelg.[119] Similarly, it was Lord Lovat's 1724 memorandum, warning of the lawlessness of the Highlands, that triggered a government investigation under General Wade into the state of Scotland's defences in 1725.[120] As a result of Wade's *Report on the State of the Highlands*, Kiliwhimen was relocated and replaced by Fort Augustus, and Fort William and Edinburgh Castle were improved, the former with basic repairs and the latter with a new enfilade curtain wall.[121]

Interest in Scotland was often dictated by current events. Domestically, the factional nature of politics frequently distracted politicians and weakened governments. The 1713–14 Bolingbroke-Harley rivalry brought an ignominious end to the War of the Spanish Succession, the 1707–30s hostility between the Squadrone and Court party (in which the Argathelians were prominent) affected the crucial first twenty-five years of Great Britain, and the enmity between George I and the Prince of Wales caused the removal of key Scottish politicians, the 2nd and later 3rd dukes of Argyll.[122] Internationally, war or peace often took Whitehall's focus from the governance of Scotland. The former made international diplomacy dominant, while the latter allowed individual interests, usually anglo-orientated, to take precedence.[123] Only when an event, such as a riot, rebellion or election was occurring, did Scotland gain significant attention. These, especially the first two, were frequently influenced by outside forces. A continental war could both distract and focus attention on Scotland, by leaving it garrisoned by troops of lesser quality, as in the '45, or by increasing fear of invasion if opponents sought to open another front to draw off British troops from continental campaigns. The latter tactic was used by France, the Jacobites' most constant and powerful ally, and Britain and Hanover's traditional enemy. This occurred in 1708 during the War of the Spanish Succession, and again for the '15. France's reticence in becoming involved in the '45 was due to recent success during the War of the Austrian Succession.[124] For similar reasons, Spain became involved in the '19 invasion but hesitated regarding the '15, '45 and the attempt in 1759, despite political and religious affiliations. For Sweden, larger-scale power politics of the Great Northern War (1700–21) put them in opposition to Hanover, and by extension, Britain. Funding domestic unrest through the Jacobites in Scotland remained a possibility until Charles XII's death in 1717, and a Royal Swedish regiment was raised for the Jacobites in 1745 but failed to join the army in Scotland.[125] Whether real or rumoured, Jacobite activity in Scotland was a major factor in deciding the attention Scotland received from the government in London.

Another significant factor that determined Whitehall's level of interest in Scotland was the attitudes and beliefs of the politicians, especially First Ministers, involved. The role of personality in shaping the political world meant that changes in power could change policy for reasons that were extraneous to Scotland itself. This contributed to the inconsistent policy towards the governance of Scotland: too much attention resulted in cries of interference, while too little led to insult, stagnation and increased support for the main alternative, the Jacobites. In chronological order, Godolphin (f. 1702–10) gave the duke of Queensbury, as Secretary of State for Scotland, a free rein.[126] His successor Robert Harley (f. 1710–14) sidelined Queensbury in an attempt to integrate the Scottish administration into Whitehall, with only limited success.[127] Walpole (f. 1722–37) ignored Scotland by devolving power to the unofficial Secretaries, the 2nd duke of Argyll, his brother, the earl of Islay, later the 3rd duke of Argyll, and their agents, the Argathelians.[128] To avoid this very dependence, which alienated the remaining Scottish elite, the duke of Newcastle (f. 1754–56) with his brother, Henry Pelham (f.c. 1741 to his death in 1754), and the duke of Hardwicke (f. 1754 to c. 1762) relied on Newcastle to take a personal role as the Secretary for Scotland in 1720–3 and 1746–54.[129] Indeed, in the aftermath of the '45, the Argathelians were viewed as too powerful and consequently their advice for leniency towards the rebels, following strategies that had proved successful following the '15, were ignored. Policies such as individual negotiations for surrender, which had broken up the command structure quickly and peacefully, and pardons based on obligations to family, friends and neighbours, were regarded with suspicion by George II, Newcastle, Hardwicke and the duke of Cumberland for placing too much power through patronage with the negotiators, chiefly the Argathelians, and encouraging the naturally nepotistic characteristic of the clans.[130]

The factionalist nature of politics and the importance of personality in gaining influence and consequently, patronage and power, meant that the personalities of the Scottish politicians of note also decided government policy and success rates of implementation. Between the Union and the '45, the duke of Queensbury (f. 1708–10) and the duke of Roxburgh (f. 1716–20) had influence and could, therefore, be effective. However, Roxburgh's influence waned in 1720–5[131] and the Marquess of Tweeddale (f. 1742–6) lacked the authority and personality to be effectual.[132]

In conclusion, the reputation of the British army in Scotland in the eighteenth century has been tarnished by many myths and half truths that have created an inaccurate image of an all-powerful, autonomous oppressive army. The intention of keeping a garrison in Scotland was to provide a military force that could prevent Jacobite unrest or invasion. This is evidenced by the creation of Britain's first domestic military infrastructure of roads and purpose-built barracks. However, the army was constrained by the law, its small size, and the inconsistent and low level of support from the government. The irregular post of Secretary of State for Scotland relied heavily on the personality and abilities of its incumbent and this meant that decisions regarding Scotland often fluctuated and were based on issues of 'power politics' or international events, rather than Scotland itself. The distance between London and Scotland, the ignorance regarding its people and their true motivations, and the lack of interest in the country's governance unless it presented a problem, all meant that policies towards Scotland were reactionary at best and absent at worst. Indeed, given this attitude from London, it is particularly striking that the level of support for the Union and protestant succession from within Scotland is so overlooked. Without such internal support, maintaining a Whig, pro-protestant succession government would have been much harder. The presence of so many Scots in the British army and in civil authority in Scotland demonstrates a greater complexity of motivations and desires than a simple unity of nationality or a policy imposed from London. This is in evidence at every level of society, from the social elite as politicians and civil servants, to the public as regular soldiers and militia or through acts such as fasting, subscriptions and celebrating anniversaries of the Hanoverian royal family. All levels actively involved themselves in the continuation of the British state. Given the number of Scottish officers and men in the British army throughout this period, it is clear that despite opposition to the Union and the rejection of the protestant succession by the Jacobites, many Scots found that service in the British army offered not only a career but a way of contributing to and influencing the British state.

Notes

1. S. Reid, *The Scottish Jacobite Army 1745–6* (Oxford, 2006), 58.
2. Such as the 1713 Bill to dissolve the Union over extensions to the Malt Tax, which failed by only four votes and the public and political outrage in response to the punishments demanded of Edinburgh in the aftermath of the Porteous Riots in 1736. A. Murdoch, *'The People Above'. Politics and Administration in Mid-Eighteenth-Century Scotland* (Edinburgh, 1980), 29 and P. Dickson, *Red John of the Battles. John, 2nd Duke of Argyll and 1st Duke of Greenwich, 1680–1743* (London, 1973), 220–1.
3. R. Wodrow, *The History of Sufferings of the Church of Scotland from the Restoration to the Revolution* (Glasgow, 1836), IV of IV, 247–9.
4. J. G. Fyfe (ed.), *Scottish Diaries and Memoirs, 1550–1746* (Stirling, 1928), 323.
5. R. Stewart, 'The Savage as Peacemaker: The Highland Host of 1678', *Scottish Tradition*, 20, 1995, 36–8.
6. A. M. Starkey, 'Robert Wodrow and The History of the Sufferings of the Church of Scotland', *Church History*, 43: 4 (1974), 488, 496.
7. G. Davies, 'The Quarters of the English Army in Scotland in 1656', *Scottish Historical Review*, 21 (1924), 63–7.
8. Ibid., 65; W. Mackay, 'General Monck's campaign in the Highlands in 1654', *Transactions of the Gaelic Society of Inverness*, 18 (1881–2), 77; H. Baker, *The Glencairn Uprising, 1653–54* (Lancaster, 2005), 5, 7, 68.
9. Davies, 'Quarters of the English', 63–7.
10. J. Black, *A Military Revolution? Military Change and European Society 1550–1800* (London, 1991), 3–4, 10, 93–4.
11. L. S. Schwoerer, *'No Standing Armies!' The antiarmy Ideology in Seventeenth-Century England* (London and Baltimore, 1974), 188–9; T. Hayter, *The army and the crowd in mid-Georgian England* (London and Basingstoke, 1978), 10–11.
12. Houlding, *Fit for Service. The training of the British Army, 1715–1795* (Oxford, 1981), 10–11.
13. C. Duffy, *The '45* (London, 2003), 132.
14. Though the exact strength varied, numbers were 2,034 foot and 650 dragoons (2,684) or 2,000 foot and 400 dragoons (2,400) Government troops versus 2,700 Jacobites (C. Duffy, *The '45* (London, 2003), 12; R. Matthews, *England Versus Scotland* (Barnsley, 2003), 232–3) or 2,300 versus 2,500 (D. Smurthwaite, *The Complete Guide to the Battlefields of Britain* (London, 1993), 201) or 2,300 versus 2,500 (W. Seymour, *Battles in Britain and their political background 1642–1746*, 2 vols, II, 1975, p. 204).
15. Duffy, *The '45*, 132.
16. National Archives of Scotland [hereafter NAS], GD220/5/568/1, Sir Robert Pollock to duke of Montrose, 7 June 1715.
17. NAS, GD220/5/568/2, 'Return of Hill and Hamilton's regiments 3 June 1715' enclosed in GD220/5/568/1, Sir Robert Pollock to duke of Montrose, 7 June 1715.
18. Duffy, *The '45*, 141.
19. Houlding, *Fit for Service*, 2, 23, 28, 59–60, 75.
20. Duffy, *The '45*, 141.
21. S. Reid, *British Redcoat 1740–1793* (Oxford, 1996), 27.
22. Duffy, *The '45*, 141.
23. Ibid., 131.
24. W. B. Blaikie, 'The First News that reached Edinburgh of the Landing of Prince Charles, 1745', *The Scottish Historical Review*, 23 (1925), 164, 166.

25. Ibid., 167.
26. Blaikie, '*First News*', 166, 170.
27. For a compelling indictment of frustrations caused by poor communications and unformed command structures, see J. Fergusson of Kilkerren, *Argyll in the Forty-Five* (London, 1951).
28. Such as the public opinion gauging conducted by Daniel Defoe prior to the Union. R. Deacon, *A History of British Secret Service* (London, 1980), 88, 90.
29. B. Harris, *Politics and the Nation. Britain in the Mid-Eighteenth Century* (Oxford, 2002), 154.
30. Bradstreet had only volunteered three months previously and his loyalty was barely tried. D. Bradstreet, *The Life and Uncommon Adventures of Capt. Dudley Bradstreet. Being the most Genuine and Extraordinary, perhaps, ever published* (Dublin, 1755), 126, 128, 131, 138.
31. Ibid., 138; R. C. Jarvis, *Collected Papers on the Jacobite Risings* (Manchester, 1972), 2 vols, II, 98–9.
32. Duffy, *The '45*, 16, 413.
33. Schwoerer, '*No Standing Armies!*', 188–9; J. Donet, *British Barracks 1600–1914. Their architecture and role in society* (Norwich, 1998), xiii, 39–40.
34. Duffy, *The '45*, 151.
35. NAS, GD220/15/568/17, Sir Robert Pollock to duke of Montrose, 24 September 1715.
36. NAS, GD220/5/568/19, Sir Robert Pollock to duke of Montrose, 28 October 1715.
37. February 1746, March 1746 and February 1746 respectively. C. Tabraham and D. Grove, *Fortress Scotland and the Jacobites* (London, 1995), 90–1; Duffy, *The '45*, 443, 447–8, 451.
38. Tabraham and Grove, *Fortress Scotland,* 90–1 and Duffy, *The '45*, 452–7, 581.
39. Donet, *British Barracks*, 17.
40. Ibid., 14, 16.
41. Houlding, *Fit for Service*, 36; Donet, *British Barracks*, 37.
42. The National Archives [hereafter TNA], SP54/6/41, Petition of Alexander McDonald of Glengary. Though dated 1714, McDonald complained that in 1704 he had a detachment of the garrison of Fort William lodged in his house and estates and was still owed £3,542 in losses and damages. Interestingly he added that this 'is directly contrary to the Law of Scotland' because it was during a time of peace.
43. Donet, *British Barracks*, 1.
44. S. Reid, *Castles and Tower Houses of the Scottish Clans 450–1650* (Oxford and New York, 2006); C. Duffy, *Fire & Stone. The Science of Fortress Warfare, 1660–1860* (London and Pennsylvania, 1996).
45. Taylor, *Military Roads,* 14.
46. Murdoch, *People Above,* 23–4.
47. A. Randall, *Riotous Assemblies: Popular Protest in Hanoverian England* (Oxford, 2006), 24–5.
48. Hayter, *Army and the crowd*, 10, 11, 16–17; Donet, *British Barracks*, 41.
49. J. H. Burton, *Lives of Simon Lord Lovat, and Duncan Forbes, of Culloden. From original sources* (London, 1847), 315–17.
50. Harris, *Politics and the Nation*, 151, 153.
51. A. Stewart, *The Trial of Archibald Stewart Esq; late Provost of Edinburgh, before the High Court of Judiciary in Scotland, For neglect of Duty, and Misbehaviour in the Execution of his Office, as Lord Provost of Edinburgh, before and at the Time the Rebels got Possession of that City in the Month of September 1745* (Edinburgh, 1747).
52. Murdoch, *People Above*, 90–1.

53. C. D. Ellestad, 'The Mutinies of 1689', *Journal of the Society for Army Historical Research*, 53, Spring 1975, 4–5, 7, 9–10, 14–15, 17, 20.
54. TNA, SP54/5/68, James Stewart, Lord Advocate of Edinburgh, to unknown, 20 May 1712, SP/54/5/92, Stewart to unknown, 14 June 1712, SP54/5/44, Stewart to unknown, 31 January 1713.
55. NAS, GD50/216/37 *Extract of the Proceedings before James Graham of Airth Esq; Judge of the High Court of Admiralty in Scotland... against Thomas McAdams, Soldier and James Lang Corporal* (London, 1737).
56. G. Holmes, *The Making of a Great Power. Late Stuart and early Georgian Britain, 1660–1722* (New York, 1993), 290; C. Whatley, *Scottish Society 1707–1830. Beyond Jacobitism, towards industrialisation* (Manchester, 2000), 147. For a list of forty-three peers who were also serving soldiers at the Union see J. S. Shaw, *The Management of Scottish Society 1701–1764* (Edinburgh, 1983), 197–8.
57. Oxford Dictionary of National Biography [hereafter ODNB], Simon Fraser, 11th Lord Lovat by Edward M. Furgol; Burton, *Lives of Simon*, 163–4, 209.
58. A. Crichton, *The Life and Diary of Lt. Col. J. Blackader* (London, 1824), 506, 514–16, 533–5, 536, 543.
59. Whatley, *Scottish Society*, 152.
60. Tabraham and Grove, *Fortress Scotland*, 61; ODNB, William Mackenzie, 5th Earl of Seaforth by Davie Horsburgh.
61. ODNB, John Dalrymple, 2nd Earl of Stair by H. M. Stevens rev. William C. Lowe; G. G. Cunningham, *A History of England in the Lives of Englishmen* (London and Edinburgh, 1853), 7 vols, IV, 157–8; P. Dickson, *Red John of the Battles. John, 2nd Duke of Argyll and 1st Duke of Greenwich, 1680–1743* (London, 1973), 96–7, 99; ODNB, John Campbell, 2nd Duke of Argyll by Alexander Murdoch.
62. G. Holmes, *Augustan England. Professions, State and Society, 1680–1730* (London, 1982), 263.
63. S. Reid, *1745. A Military History of the Last Jacobite Rising* (Staplehurst, 2001), 85.
64. I. H. Mackay Scobie, 'The Highland Independent Companies of 1745–1747', reprinted from Spring 1941 issue of *Journal of the Society for Army Historical Research*, 12–14.
65. Burton, *Lives of Simon*, 115–17, 195; A. Fergusson (ed.), *Major Fraser's Manuscript. His Adventures in Scotland and England; His Mission to, and Travels in, France in Search of his Chief; his Services in the Rebellion (and his Quarrels) with Simon Fraser, Lord Lovat 1696–1737* (Edinburgh, 1889), 2 vols, II, 83–4; ODNB, William Mackenzie, 5th Earl of Seaforth by Davie Horsburgh.
66. Mackay Scobie, 'Highland Independent Companies', 25–6; ODNB, George Mackenzie, 3rd Earl of Cromartie by Murray G. H. Pittock.
67. P. Simpson, *The Independent Highland Companies 1603–1760* (Edinburgh, 1996), 92–3; Burton, *Lives of Simon*, 117.
68. Mackay Scobie, 'Highland Independent Companies', 12.
69. B. Lenman, *The Jacobite Clans of the Great Glen, 1650–1784* (Dalkeith, 2004), 116, 118, 123–4, 126–8.
70. Both real power and the power the clan perceived him to have were of vital importance to Lovat. His opinions are clearly expressed about the propaganda he wrote for his father's memorial (Burton, *Lives of Simon*, 160–1).
71. Simpson, *Independent Highland Companies*, 113; Burton, *Lives of Simon*, 118; B. Lenman, *The Jacobite Clans of the Great Glen, 1650–1784* (Dalkeith, 2004), 102; ODNB, Simon Fraser, 11th Lord Lovat by Edward M. Furgol.

72. R. Mitchison, 'The government and the Highlands, 1707–1745' in N. T. Phillipson and R. Mitchison (eds), *Scotland in the Age of Improvement. Essays in Scottish History in the Eighteenth Century* (Edinburgh, 1970), 28.
73. W. C. Mackenzie, *Simon Fraser, Lord Lovat. His life and times* (London, 1908), 322–3.
74. Fergusson, *Argyll in the Forty-Five*, 24.
75. Burton, *Lives of Simon*, 377; Reid, *1745*, 85. The Macdonalds of Sleat and the Macleods of Skye received two companies each. See Mackay Scobie, 'Highland Independent Companies', 12.
76. Burton, *Lives of Simon*, 373.
77. F. McLynn, *The Jacobites* (London, 1988), 80.
78. P. Laslett (ed.), *Patriarcha and other political works of Sir Robert Filmer* (Oxford, 1949), 11–14.
79. George to William, 24 March 1746 and William to George, 26 March 1746; K. Tomasson, *The Jacobite General* (Edinburgh and London, 1958), 190.
80. B. Lenman, *The Jacobite Risings in Britain 1689–1746* (London, 1984), 256–7; Duffy, *The '45*, 50; D. Szechi, *The Jacobites: Britain and Europe, 1688–1788* (Manchester, 1994), 23.
81. NLS MS.16604 (107) and MS 16604(108), earl of Kilmarnock to 'Dearest Nanny' [Anne, Countess of Kilmarnock], 15 October 1745 and 18 October 1745.
82. Murdoch, *People Above*, 4.
83. J. Black, *A Military Revolution? Military Change and European Society 1550–1800* (London, 1991), 78; I. F. Burton and A. N. Newman, 'Sir John Cope: Promotion in the Eighteenth-Century Army', *English Historical Review*, 78: 309 (1963), 668.
84. K. M. Brown, 'From Scottish Lords to British Officers: State Building, Elite Integration and the Army in the Seventeenth Century' in N. MacDougall (ed.) *Scotland and War* (Edinburgh, 1991), 141–5.
85. R. M. Barnes, *A History of the Regiments and Uniforms of the British Army* (London, 1950), 26–8, 33.
86. Brown, 'From Scottish Lords', 147–9; Houlding, *Fit for Service*, 172. At the Battle of Blenheim, for example, the earl of Orkney's Regiment of Foot served alongside Marlborough's 1st Regiment of Foot, three years before the Union.
87. D. McBane, *The Expert Sword-Man's Companion Or the True Art of Self-defence. With An Account of the Authors Life, And his Transactions during the Wars With France. To Which is Annexed, The Art of Gunnerie By Donald McBane* (Glasgow, 1728), 25–6.
88. M. Macintosh, *A History of Inverness. Being a narrative of the historical events, mainly military, concerning the town and round about, from the earliest times until the early Victorian period* (Inverness, 1939), 119.
89. Duffy, *The '45*, 131.
90. McBane, *Expert Sword-Man's*, 26; J. White, *The Cameronians (Scottish Rifles) in France* (Glasgow, 1917), 9–10; ODNB, Sir Thomas Livingstone by H. M. Chichester, rev. Timothy Harrison Place.
91. Duffy, *The '45*, 151, 514, 578.
92. A. Crichton, *The Life and Diary of Lt. Col. J. Blackader* (London, 1824), 462–3, 466–9, 471–2; D. Szechi, *1715. The Great Jacobite Rebellion* (New Haven and London, 2006), 122.
93. Szechi, *1715*, 119, 126.
94. Harris, *Politics and the Nation*, 578.
95. A. Carlyle, *Autobiography of the Rev. Dr Alexander Carlyle Minister of Inveresk Containing Memorials of the Men and Event of his time* (Edinburgh and London, 1860), 128, 132–4, 139.

96. Harris, *Politics and the Nation*, 151.
97. Brown, 'From Scottish Lords', 148–9.
98. J. Hayes, 'Scottish Officers in the Army, 1714–63', *Scottish Historical Review*, 37 (1958), 26.
99. John Rylands Library, Bagshawe MSS 2/2/141. Lt. William Dawkin of 39th Regiment, December 1747.
100. H. T. Dickinson (ed.), *A Companion to Eighteenth-century Britain* (Oxford, 2002), 476.
101. R. Clyde, *From Rebel to Hero. The Image of the Highlander, 1745–1830* (East Linton, 1995), 150.
102. W. Roughead (ed.), *The Trial of Captain Porteous* (Glasgow and Edinburgh, 1909), 34, 36–7, 43.
103. Wodrow, *History of Sufferings*, 172–3 and A. M. Starkey, 'Robert Wodrow and The History of the Sufferings of the Church of Scotland', *Church History* 43:4 (1974), 495.
104. J. Oates, *Sweet William or The Butcher? The Duke of Cumberland and the '45* (Barnsley, 2008), 28; A. Starkey, *War in the Age of Enlightenment, 1700–1789* (London, 2003), 149–50.
105. In only the week after Culloden, five notices were made against plundering and disorder, and one court martial held to punish transgressors. British Library, Hardwicke Papers, Vol. DCCCCIX, Joseph Yorke's Order Book, Add 36257 f. 60, 62, 64, 68, 69, 71; Starkey, *War in the Age*, 5.
106. Houlding, *Fit for Service*, 2, 23, 28, 59–60, 75.
107. Davies, 'Quarters of the English Army', 63–7; Houlding, *Fit for Service*, 75, 77.
108. McBane, *Expert Sword-Man's*, 25.
109. Simpson, *Independent Highland Companies*, 92–3.
110. J. L. Roberts, *The Jacobite Wars. Scotland and the Military Campaigns of 1715 and 1745* (Edinburgh, 2002), 65, 193; D. Stewart, *Sketches of the character, manners, and present state of the Highlanders of Scotland* (Edinburgh, 1825), 293–4.
111. Duffy, *The '45*, 141–2.
112. H. Bland, *A treatise of military discipline; in which is laid down and explained the duty of the officer and soldier, Thro' the several Branches of the Service. By Humphrey Bland, Esq; Adjutant-General; and Colonel of one of His Majesty's Regiments of Dragoons* (Dublin, 1743), 116–31, especially 116–17.
113. Reid, *1745*, 148; Duffy, *The '45*, 511.
114. Houlding, *Fit for Service*, 59–60, 75.
115. Murdoch, *People Above*, 1, 4, 27.
116. Ibid., 5.
117. Harris, *Politics and the Nation*, 151.
118. Tabraham and Grove, *Fortress Scotland*, 56.
119. Donet, *British Barracks*, 20.
120. Burton, *Lives of Simon*, 179–80.
121. Taylor, *Military Roads*, 18 and Tabraham and Grove, *Fortress Scotland*, 65, 70, 78, 81–5.
122. ODNB, Archibald Campbell, 3rd Duke of Argyll by Alexander Murdoch; Murdoch, *People Above*, 30.
123. R. Mitchison, 'The government and the Highlands, 1707–1745' in N. T. Phillipson and R. Mitchison (eds), *Scotland in the Age of Improvement. Essays in Scottish History in the Eighteenth Century* (Edinburgh, 1970), 24; Murdoch, *People Above*, 22.
124. Significantly, French victory at Fontenoy (11 May 1745) came just prior to Jacobite preparations for the '45. Szechi, *The Jacobites*, 54–7, 96–7.

125. J. J. Murray, 'Sweden and the Jacobites in 1716', *Huntington Library Quarterly*, 8:3 (May 1945), 260–1; F. McLynn, *The Jacobites* (London, 1988), 40–2; R. I. Frost, *The Northern Wars, 1558–1721* (Harlow, 2000), 295.
126. Murdoch, *People Above*, 28–9.
127. Ibid., 29.
128. Ibid., 19, 31, 32.
129. Ibid., 6, 10, 19.
130. M. Sankey, *Jacobite Prisoners of the 1715 Rebellion. Preventing and Punishing Insurrection in Early Hanoverian Britain* (Aldershot, 2005), 100–2, 150, 154–5; British Library, Newcastle Papers Add.MS.32707 ff. 13 Cumberland to Newcastle, 4 April 1746; Add.MS.32707 ff. 87, Cumberland to Newcastle, 23 April 1746; Oates, *Sweet William*, 62, 143, 162.
131. Murdoch, *People Above*, 6.
132. ODNB, John Hay, 4th Marquess of Tweeddale by Richard Scott.

A CONTESTED EIGHTEENTH-CENTURY ELECTION: BANFFSHIRE, 1795

ALISTAIR MUTCH

they advanced, upon the day of the contest, at the head of nine as good men of parchment as ever took the oath of trust and possession.[1]

Walter Scott's waspish comments on the duplicities of Scottish lawyers in creating freeholders 'by dint of clipping and paring here, adding and eiking there' in *Guy Mannering* were, of course, set in south west Scotland.[2] However, conflict over the nature of the oath of trust and possession, which was designed to be the test of the right of a freeholder to a vote, also figured largely in the conduct and aftermath of the 1795 Banffshire election. Patrick points out that contested elections in the north east in the eighteenth century were rare, because of the ability of rich landowners to manipulate the franchise.[3] The 1795 by-election in Banffshire was one which has attracted limited attention, in part because of a subsequent general election which made the result a little academic. In his overview of the representation of the constituency, Thorne notes a number of parties manoeuvring for position in the early 1790s. Two of these contested the by-election and, based on the evidence available, Thorne observes that, 'It is not clear how far Duff persisted, and McDowall Grant was returned'.[4] However, Colonel Duff of Carnousie did indeed persist in pushing his claim to a vote. More than this, he then brought a private prosecution, with the support of the 'Banffshire Association' (and the concordance of the Lord Advocate, Robert Dundas) for perjury on the part of one elector, a prosecution in which the 'oath of trust and possession' occupied centre stage. This trial and the records it generated give us some insight into both the election and the manoeuvring which preceded it. Together with other archival material they point to a challenge to aristocratic dominance on the part of a new class of improving landowners no longer willing to accept a feudal lead.

Scott's concern with electoral corruption echoed earlier disquiet with what was seen as the corrupting influence of wealth and luxury on Scottish political life, especially that emanating from India. Such concern, articulated by Henry

Mackenzie in the pages of the *Lounger*, has been seen by Dwyer and Murdoch as the means by which Henry Dundas was able to build his political power.[5] This was by giving voice to the concerns of the country gentry in the face of growing aristocratic wealth. Their resentment took shape in campaigns, reflected in county meetings, to reform the franchise. The case of the Banffshire by-election gives an ironic twist to such campaigns. For fighting the cause of the smaller landowners against the wealth and might of the Earl of Fife was a man who had made his fortune in India. This article explores the paradox. It firstly outlines the key *dramatis personae*, notably the Earl of Fife and Colonel Patrick 'Tiger' Duff. It then outlines the challenge which Duff's candidature posed and how it was followed up before the High Court of Justiciary. Although Duff's challenge was ultimately unsuccessful, it sheds light on the rise of a new faction claiming elite status and, in particular, on the estrangement of Fife's factor, William Rose from his former master. It also provides material for more tenuous speculation on the influence of Duff's action on Scott's fiction.

James Duff, second Lord Fife (1729–1809), dominated Banffshire politically and economically in the second half of the eighteenth century.[6] He served as member of Parliament for the county between 1754 and 1784 before his place was taken by his illegitimate son James. Fife continued as the member for Elginshire until 1790, when his persistent lobbying for a British peerage was granted and he moved to the Lords. A man used to getting his own way, he fell out with his son over his support for the opposition in the dispute over the Regency and forced him to give way to Sir James Ferguson of Pitfour. This caused some disquiet to otherwise loyal supporters such as Andrew Hay of Rannes, but in 1790 when Ferguson moved to Aberdeenshire, Fife managed to get Sir James Grant, husband of his niece, returned. However, the disquiet about his manipulation of the vote increased and was to boil over when Grant later resigned his position, as will be seen below.

Fife was able to maintain his control because of the notoriously limited and corrupt nature of the eighteenth century Scottish franchise.[7] Indeed, Fife was one of the first to object at a meeting in Edinburgh in 1775 to efforts to reform the franchise, arguing that they infringed on the rights of property. In response Henry Dundas retorted

> That the printing and making known the bill, could only be opposed by those who were afraid of the sentiments of the gentlemen of the country, and who had changed the constitutional method of gaining votes by hospitality and good offices, into the modern mode of creating fictious votes without any real property; a practice the noble Lord who spoke before him was well acquainted with.[8]

As we will see, Dundas' allegations seem to have carried a good deal of weight. At the heart of Scott's fictional treatment was the ability of lawyers to manipulate liferents of feudal superiorities to grant votes. Two pieces of legislation in 1714 and 1734 sought to curb such practices, but with little success. They enabled a test to be put to freeholders claiming a vote at the annual Michaelmass meeting which established the electoral roll based on their swearing an 'oath of trust and possession' that confirmed their true and independent basis for the franchise.[9] However, there was little provision for enforcement, as will be seen. This meant that the already narrow franchise could easily be manipulated by larger landowners with superiorities which could be granted to those who would vote the right way. Periodic challenges were made to the make up of electoral rolls and the Banffshire roll was reduced from 108 electors in 1790 to 39 in 1794.

Fife was also, however, a strong supporter of the Union and the British constitution in an area which had still recent memories of the 1745 rising, in which large numbers of Banffshire gentry were implicated.[10] One of the leading figures in the rising, Andrew Hay of Rannes, who was excluded from the Act of Indemnity but eluded capture for several years before escaping to exile in France, only died in 1789.[11] Fife had made considerable efforts to secure him a pardon, which was only granted in 1780. Hay's will is interesting in pointing to the network of local figures in which Fife was implicated. Charles Hay, advocate, acted as proxy executor on behalf of Fife, to whom a balance of money was to be lent until Rannes' affairs were settled. The other executors were Alexander Gordon of Cairnbanno and Letterfourie, Andrew Hay of Mountblairy and William Rose of Ballivat.[12] Gordon was 'out' in the '45 and escaped to help run the family wine business in Madeira. He was an important connection with Patrick Duff, as will be seen below. Andrew Hay was the son of George Hay of Mountblairy, brother in law of Fife, and taken prisoner before Culloden. Rose was Fife's main factor and had strong connections to many of the gentry in Banffshire. He was a loyal confidant and functionary to Fife until a spectacular fall out around 1795.[13]

Fife was, therefore, an important part of the established governance structures, but his relationships with the 'manager' of Scottish political affairs, Henry Dundas, were prickly.[14] Fife's main objective above all was to preserve his independence of action, but Dundas was concerned not to allow him complete dominance in the north east.[15] Accordingly, Dundas engineered a rather unwilling alliance between Fife and the Duke of Gordon in 1787. The test of this came in 1793, when Fife, having become reconciled to his son James, sought to press his claims to be returned again for Banffshire at the next poll, but Dundas wanted him to support William Grant of Beldornie. Dundas complained that he and Pitt 'have both an accurate recollection of all the professions your lordship made to us at the time you solicited a British peerage, and we find it difficult to reconcile them with the reception you have given to the first opportunity you have had of manifesting the sincerity of them.'[16] It was following this intervention that Thorne notes

> There were apparently three other aspirants to the seat, who manoeuvred for position during the next two years: Abercromby, Col. Patrick ('Tiger') Duff of

Carnousie, an East India officer currently on furlough, and David McDowall Grant, a Renfrewshire man who had married a Banffshire heiress. In January 1795 the latter told his brother that he was the best placed, but that Duff of Carnousie was a major threat.[17]

This introduces the other major character in the events of 1795, a man with strong ties to Fife but one who was to be pitted against him for a number of years. Patrick Duff (1742–1803) was the son of a tenant farmer, John Duff.[18] However, John was not without his connections and in later life was a correspondent with Fife on agricultural matters.[19] His son, who pursued a military career, was also grateful for the intervention of his aristocratic patron. In 1776 he wrote to Fife thanking him for a letter he had written to General Clavering on his behalf and for 'the friendly and polite treatment I experienced [from] you when in Europe' and again when leaving the country to return to India in 1790 'thanking your Lordship for your great and flattering attentions which I shall remember with great pleasure'.[20] However, the more significant connection was with his uncles James and Alexander Gordon of Letterfourie. Successful wine merchants in Madeira, they took a keen interest in the education and careers of their nephews. The eldest nephew, James, was educated with a view to a career in the Madeira wine business, with his brothers Patrick, William and John being destined for military careers. They joined so many other Scots in the service of the East India Company, with Patrick being by far the most successful of them.[21]

After initial service from 1760 as a 'gentleman volunteer' with the 89th Regiment of Foot, Patrick transferred on the disbanding of the regiment in 1763 to the East India Company's artillery. He rose to the rank of captain by 1766, being mentioned in despatches for his conduct at the battle of Buxar, but his military career nearly came to an abrupt end in 1766. In that year, the Company sought to withdraw the payment of double 'batta' or living expenses for European officers in the field. A combination of officers vowed to resign simultaneously from the service unless double batta was restored, and Duff was a particularly vigorous advocate of this policy. Knowledge of the combination came to light when Duff was found to have set light to a fellow officer's quarters: 'it appeared that the dispute arose from ensign Davis's refusing to give up his commission to captain Duff, who would have forced it from him.'[22] Perhaps this was inspired by folk memories of the tactics his Jacobite forebears had used to encourage the unwilling, but it certainly seems to suggest a somewhat hot-headed and determined character. Duff was court martialled, and dismissed the service, returning to Scotland.

However, he managed to secure some influence, perhaps from Fife, in order to return. It was on his next tour of duty that he obtained his soubriquet of 'Tiger'. When out hunting he was attacked by a tiger and pinned to the ground. The rest of his party having fled, Duff was able to remove the bayonet from his rifle and stab the tiger through the heart. He then managed to walk back to camp, surprising all by his escape. He carried the scar on his cheek for the rest of his life making him, given his height of six feet four inches, a formidable figure in his later years to the children of Banff.[23] He was obviously a person of significant physical presence, as well as possessing considerable courage. He also seems to have been an extremely effective artillery officer. He returned to Scotland again in 1774 to marry his first cousin Ann Duff, but she was to die on the return voyage to India, in 1776. Duff rose during this tour of duty, which finished in 1788, to the rank of colonel. It was also during this period that Duff seems to have made his fortune. For many officers this came through prize money or from selling their services to local rulers, but for Patrick it came from his family contacts in the Madeira wine trade. In 1778 James Duff wrote to his uncle James Gordon at Letterfourie enclosing a proposal from his brother suggesting that if they could persuade sea captains to transport wine to Calcutta he would

> pay them a price in proportion to what other wines sell for in this country... which I should think would be a great advantage to them, [for]... any person who brings goods for sale here ought to be very glad to have the certainty of an immediate sale at the market price, as some have of late been obliged to leave effects unsold in the country, at great loss and risque.[24]

This seems to have paid off, for by 1789 Patrick was looking to buy an estate back in his native north east. He had returned to Scotland the previous year and wrote from Letterfourie to ask for Fife's advice. Those returning from India were popularly known to have extensive funds to command but Duff was determined not to pay over the odds:

> altho' I want an estate and particularly in this country, I would not give more for one than my friends thought prudent and reasonable. I know there is an idea that people from India will give more than any person else, but I assure your Lordship this is not the case with me, as I am determined to be guided by the advice of my friends in cases of this kind where I am no judge myself.[25]

Fife's brother in law George Hay of Mountblairy had been in financial trouble for some time, having sought to dispose of parts of his estate since his return from exile after the '45.[26] Fife suggested that he did not have much influence over Hay, but that Carnousie was 'the most desirable part for Col. Duff to purchase: there is a great deal of good ground and great deal to improve.'[27] Accordingly the estate was purchased with the assistance of the Gordons of Letterfourie and William Rose, Fife's factor, who acted for many whose work took them far from Banff. Having secured his new estate, Duff returned to India in 1790, pausing to have his portrait painted by George Romney in London.[28]

Patrick played a significant role in the campaign against Tipu Sultan.[29] Now in complete control of the Bengal artillery, he was appointed commanding officer of Bangalore after its capture in 1792. There he rebuilt the capacity of the siege train which was to depart to invest the fortress of Seringapatam. 'Such were the improvements introduced by the colonel', argued Major Dirom (of Muiresk near Turriff) in his account of the war, 'or acquired by experience during the war, that this unwieldy department moved with nearly as much ease as any other part of the army'.[30] However, Duff failed to receive the promotion which he felt was his due and returned to Scotland yet again in 1793. He appears to have had a strong streak of stubbornness and a keen sense of what he was entitled to, factors which might have a bearing on the account which follows. Having established his social position through the purchase of Carnousie, he proceeded to cement it by marrying Dorothea Hay of Mountblairy, sister of his neighbour Andrew Hay, himself embarking on a military career of some distinction. This brought Duff into the centre of the political intrigues which were to pitch him against Fife.

Initially, however, Duff seemed to be an ally rather than an opponent of the Fife cause. In 1793 an analysis of voting intentions sent to Pitt contains his name under the heading of 'Lord Fife's Friends (alongside the name of Lieutenant James Fyfe, the significance of which will become clear later) whilst Andrew Hay is noted under the heading 'Association to oppose Mr William Grant'.[31] At this stage, therefore, he does not seem to have posed a threat to Fife. In Rose's eyes rather the reverse was true. In August of the same year he wrote to Fife that 'Col. Duff would be a Man more to my wishes and I think you could make him firm by preliminary to Mr Pitt, tho indifferent to Mr Dundas'.[32] He continued with the optimistic forecast that 'we may prophesise a Downfall to Ministry, that Mr D is to continue with his power is impossible and a change of his Northern Department I think is unavoidable'. His closing – somewhat cryptic – flourish was

> Col Duff I hear is tired of —— and if he would take his Money that place would be —— and his house and Farm ——. Your Lordship indulging this might make him pleased with the Country, and give joy to those who esteem him [blanks in original].[33]

That Rose was close to Duff seems to receive some confirmation from an earlier letter to him in 1790 from Alexander Gordon at Letterfourie noting the 'desire of Mrs Robinson, W.R.'s mother-in-law, to continue to live in the house of Carnousie for a year but regret that major repairs are to be carried out during the summer'.[34] However, matters seemed to have changed when Fife wrote to Dundas in 1794 asserting his loyalty to the government and his intention to support Grant.[35] This seemed to fling Patrick into the arms of the Banffshire Association.

The Association was designed to counter the influence of Fife by grouping together the 'independent' freeholders of the county in a voting bloc. Of course, by the very act of association in order to dent the independence of Fife they had to sacrifice a portion of their own, a contradiction made much of in subsequent proceedings. Electing Sir George Abercromby of Birkenbogs as their convenor, the group declared

> We engage and promise, at the ensuing general election, or the first Vacancy for this County, to adhere to one another, and All to give our votes for the same person to represent the County in Parliament; And in case we shall not at first be unanimous, the Minority shall give up, and follow the Majority of the Association. And if any person upon the Roll of freeholders, who is not a Member of this Association, should stand a Candidate at the Election, it is expressly understood and declared, that the Minority (if there be one) are bound not to give their votes for such Candidate[36]

They further agreed to attend meetings and vote as a block in challenges to the electoral qualifications. In particular, they agreed to use the oath of trust and possession as a key weapon in establishing title. The group initially included David McDowall Grant of Arndilly as well as Andrew Hay of Mountblairy, John Innes of Edingight, William Leslie of Dunlugas and Peter Garden of Troup. It was this group that Duff joined and which selected Abercromby as its initial candidate. Abercromby later decided not to press his candidature and McDowall Grant came forward in his place. However, Duff was also pressing his candidature and when Fife appeared to cast his weight behind McDowall Grant, the latter broke ranks with the Association, giving rise to the contested election of 1795.

This saw an election meeting in which every step was contested. On entering the meeting in Banff on 24 July 1795 Duff alleged that several who were attending 'were not real and Independent freeholders, but a part of those Nominal and fictitious voters who had some years before been Obtruded on the County, for the purpose of increasing the political Interest of a Noble Lord who possesses an extensive Estate in that district'.[37] The majority of those attending elected McDowall Grant as *preses* (chair) with a casting vote.[38] Duff immediately objected to the title of Lieutenant James Fyfe and required that he take the oath of trust and possession immediately. However, Alexander Duff of Echt, a Grant supporter, argued that they should move to purging the roll and this was carried. There then followed a round of challenge and counter-challenge, resulting in some of those who had voted for the chair having their names expunged from the roll. One of those who took the oath and so preserved his vote was Lieutenant Fyfe. The vote was then taken with the following result, Duff securing the support of the Association:

Grant	**Duff**
Alexander Duff of Echt	Sir George Abercromby of Birkenbog
William Rose of Balival	Andrew Hay of Mountblairy
Sir James Duff of Kinstair	William Leslie of Dunlugas
James Leslie of Kinovie	John Innes of Edengeith
Lieutenant James Fyfe	Colonel Duff

Major Alex Duff of Mayen
Francis Stewart of Lesmudie
David McDowall Grant of Arndilly
John Duff of Drummuir

Francis Garden of Troup
John Gordon of Avochie

Duff was on his feet immediately, with the minutes recording:

> And Colonel Duff stated, that he considered himself duly elected Preses [presumably because Grant's election to the position was on the basis of voters whose claims had subsequently been invalidated], therefore entitled to the casting vote and declared that in the event of there proving to be an equality of voices, he took the casting vote to himself. And Colonel Duff likeways Protests that the Majority of legal votes on the Roll has been given in his favour, that he is therefore duly elected and ought to be returned.[39]

The meeting, unsurprisingly, disagreed with him and declared Grant returned. They then proceeded to ratify a revised electoral roll with thirty-six names on it. Whether the low turnout in this election was because some feared the challenge of Duff and the Association, choosing to avoid confrontation, or because it was widely known that a general election would soon be in the offing is not clear.

However, Duff was not prepared to let the result lie. The conventional way of challenging an electoral result was to present a petition to Parliament, but Duff argued that a dissolution was so close that such a course of action was not worth pursuing. Instead, with the support of the Association and the 'concordance' of the Lord Advocate, Robert Dundas, he brought a private criminal prosecution against one of the electors, Lieutenant James Fyfe of Edinglassie, for perjury, on the grounds that

> he the said James Fyfe did swear and Subscribe wilfully and falsely, and well knowing that the foresaid lands of Turtory, for which he claimed a right to vote, as aforesaid, were not actually in his possession and did not really and truly belong to him, and were not his own proper Estate, and that his Title to the said lands and estate was Nominal and fictitious, created or reserved in him in Order to enable him to Vote for a Member to serve in Parliament.[40]

It is from the evidence presented in the pursuit of this suit that we can trace the course of the election and the arguments that followed. In considering such arguments we can use the evidence presented to look at the case in three ways: for the course of the action; for what the evidence presented seems to suggest about the conduct of politics; and for what the process of the trial tells us about shifting attitudes.

Much of the extensive information presented to the court in order to consider whether to proceed to trial (around a hundred pages on each side) was concerned with the grounds on which a private prosecution could be brought. For Duff, it was argued that the Lord Advocate took no action in allegations of false oaths because of fear of being seen to be politically partial and so a private prosecution was the only means of holding offenders to account. This line of argument reveals the weakness in the legislation in providing no clear grounds for enforcement. Much of the defence's case was taken up with legal arguments about the validity of the grounds for a private prosecution and in particular with the status of the Association. Their strategy also seemed to rest on delaying proceedings for as long as possible, with Fife in particular pleading a variety of pressing circumstances preventing his examination.[41] However, the judges decided that there was a case to answer so as to 'Allow the Pannel a proof of all facts and circumstances that May tend to exculpate him or alleviate his guilt' and the case was eventually heard in June 1797.[42] In the meantime Duff had been ordered back to India and had to ask the court for permission to proceed in his absence. His advocates called eight witnesses, including William Rose and Fife. The evidence they gave orally was not recorded, but a passage in the information laid by the defence suggests why the outcome of the trial was a decision by the jury of 'not proven'. This argued with regard to the oath that 'It is therefore a secret understanding, an affection of the Mind; and when a man swears that he considers himself not to be a nominal and fictitious voter, he takes an oath of opinion.'[43] The oath, therefore, was worthless and any action which rested on it was doomed to failure. However, whilst the formal result might have gone against Duff, an examination of the evidence produced does seem to vindicate his claims, or at least arouse considerable suspicions about Fyfe's claims.

Fyfe was a lieutenant in the army but was reduced to half pay following the end of the American War of Independence. With six children he needed another source of income and was appointed as factor over Lord Fife's lands in Balvenie. In 1786 Fyfe received a liferent of a feudal superiority over some lands in Turtory and was enrolled as a freeholder at the Michaelmass 1787 meeting in Banff. However, in his absence, his name was struck out in 1792 on the grounds that he was not a real and independent freeholder. He appealed to the Court of Session, with his expenses being paid by Fife, and was reinstated. He did not receive any of the duties to which he was entitled to until the day before the 1795 poll, when he received nine years' duties from one of Fife's factors. The prosecution case was that all these transactions were purely fictitious and pointed to the evidence gained, after a considerable delay, from Fife's account books to support their case.[44] These extracts do seem to indicate that all the expenses of making up the claim and maintaining it were met by Fife. The Lieutenant was singularly unable to shed any light on these transactions, seeming to be unable in his disposition given at Keith in December 1795 to the Sheriff Substitute to remember any significant details. He could not, for example, recall how much or how he had paid for his title and had no receipt for the transaction. He thought that he must have paid for the appeal to the Court of Session, although he had no recollection of how this might have been done.[45] What he was able to produce was a letter from himself to William Rose in November 1786 which noted that Lord Fife had directed you to expedite the proper titles for establishing a qualification in my person as a Freeholder in this County. As I am certain neither his Lordship nor you would desire me to do anything that was not legal I shall therefore accept of the qualification upon the terms you write of[46]

A further letter from Fife to Rose in May the following year was produced which declared:

I therefore desire you will table with any friends that I have disponed qualifications to, and that I desire they will bind themselves by their Word of honour during their life, or until a Wadset is redeemed by the regular course of law, that they will Never give back the Vote to Me nor My heirs.[47]

These letters do seem to be establishing a degree of cover, for the telling part of Fyfe's admission is

That he does not recollect how often he has Voted as a Freeholder at an Election, but remembers once voted for Pitfour – and on this occasion he thinks he gave his vote to Pitfour at the request of Mr Rose, but thinks he received a letter from Pitfour himself soliciting his Vote. That he voted at last Election in Banffshire for W. MacDowall Grant and was requested to do so by W. Rose and that Lord Fife also mentioned to him, that he was rather Interested for Mr MacDowall Grant and if the Declarant was not Engaged it would be agreeable to give Mr MacDowall Grant his support.[48]

Given the way in which all his expenses had been met, his dependence on Fife for his livelihood (although he was removed as factor in 1795) and the evasive nature of his evidence, there do seem to be grounds for suspicion, something compounded by what Dundas felt about Fife's skill in manipulating the franchise.[49]

Such suspicion was not sufficient, however, to obtain a conviction. Duff was perhaps to some extent unfortunate in his timing. It was not long since the courts at Edinburgh had been the venue for the infamous sedition trials and this was much played upon by Fyfe's defence team.[50] In their initial information they argued that

We all know, that within these few years past, a general spirit of reform arose, and such has been its horrible effects in some countries, and its pernicious tendency in our own, that it is devoutly to be wished it may never again exhibit its sonorous enchantment. Even the wisest and best men were not free from its contagion, and exceeded in order to do what they thought was good. A violent outcry arose against qualifications by way of liferent and wadset, and numbers of people thought they could not do enough to abolish them.[51]

This rhetoric did not seem to disturb the judge, who ruled that there was a case to answer, but it may have found its way into the courtroom proceedings. What is striking, however, is that given this background Duff persisted and that in doing so he forced the Earl of Fife into the witness box. Given his father's close connections and the patronage which it appears that Fife exercised on his behalf this was a considerable about-turn. Part of this might be attributed to Duff's forthright character but another part might represent a shift in the balance of local politics, with newly wealthy smaller landowners, especially those with status from their military exploits, being more willing to challenge the exercise of power by men like Fife. As Dwyer and Murdoch point out, this willingness had its roots in the 1770s when 'the opposition of many small and substantial landowners to the practice of nominal voting grew fierce'.[52] The ironic twist in the Banffshire case was that it took the wealth of India (and perhaps a certain stubbornness born out of military service there) to crystallise this resentment. In Ferguson's view, this was hardly a democratic challenge. As he says, the challenges to such power came from the fringes and were concerned with the righting of glaring abuses, rather than wholesale reform. 'Such movements as arose', he observes, 'were not popular and were in no sense radical or democratic'.[53] However, this may not have been how matters appeared to Fife.

His correspondence with his chief factor, William Rose, gives ample evidence of his reactionary opinions. His response to the Church and King riots at Birmingham in 1791 was to wish that the mob had been able to get hold of Priestley and 'cut out his ears'.[54] He had 'always told you what would happen' if duties to God and man were subverted. He returned to the topic in the following year, urging his factor to 'Resist all reforms. You have always heard my invincible opinion they come from Levellers, who only wish to get up a few steps to pull down the whole fabrick'.[55] Finally, in 1794 Fife wrote somewhat cryptically

> All these vile papers that your friend the Doctor sends to the Country has a wonderful bad effect, I wonder common sense teaches not every wise man to check all levelling of God, man and every society.[56]

Who 'the Doctor' was is not clear, but in 1795 there was a rupture between Fife and his factor which stemmed the flow of correspondence. The Taylers, writing from their position as descendants of Fife, are at a loss to explain why a relationship of forty years should have broken down in spectacular fashion. Part of the clue might rest in the way Rose was treated as a social inferior, Fife making much at the ensuing trial of the way in which he had rescued Rose from obscurity. However, his correspondence indicates the way in which he was accustomed to speaking to Rose. A sample is his request that Rose find him somebody trained in looking after fruit: 'Now do stir your fat personage and see to find out such a treasure'.[57] This can be taken, of course, as good natured joshing, but when we go further back we find passages like this about Rose's cousin:

> I hope you will be at great pains with the young man and don't learn him to lay a-bed in the morning. If you make him acquainted with business, I will take some pains to learn him to serve properly when I take him, but before I

see him, you must take every Drop of the Mother's Milk and Country pride out of his nose. You know I had a pretty good quantity to take out of your own, and I will do you justice you are pretty well now.[58]

Is it too much to speculate that the split, coming about the same time as Duff's challenge to Fife's electoral power, was the culmination of resentment about this type of treatment? We have noted how much Rose estimated Duff's potential and that he had personal connections with him. It may be that Duff's challenge, although unsuccessful, was a catalyst to Rose and others who resented dominance based on outmoded feudal principles.

Duff returned from India for the last time in 1797 with the rank of Major General. He never challenged for political power again and was not to enjoy his Carnousie estate for long. In 1801 his brother James, the Madeira wine merchant, failed, leaving Patrick to cover his debts. This meant that he left an encumbered estate to pass on to his son when he died together with his wife in Edinburgh in 1803.[59] It is interesting to speculate, though, that his actions may have provided Walter Scott with some of his material for *Guy Mannering*. Scott was active as an advocate in Edinburgh in the years 1792 to 1797 and, given his interest in Indian affairs and their impact on Scotland, can hardly have been unaware of the trial of Lieutenant Fyfe and its implications.[60] The trial gives us an insight into the unsettling influence of Indian wealth on established patterns of life in Scotland and a practical example of how electoral corruption worked.

Notes

My thanks to members of staff at Aberdeen University Special Libraries and Archives and at the National Archives of Scotland.

1. Walter Scott, *Guy Mannering* (London, 2003), 32.
2. Ibid.
3. J. Patrick, 'The 1806 election in Aberdeenshire', *Northern Scotland*, 1(2) (1973), 151–76.
4. R. G. Thorne, *The House of Commons 1790–1820, Vol. 2, Constituencies* (London, 1986), 521.
5. John Dwyer and Alexander Murdoch, 'Paradigms and politics: manners, morals and the rise of Henry Dundas, 1770–1784' in Jon Dwyer, Roger Mason and Alexander Murdoch, *New perspectives on the politics and culture of early modern Scotland* (Edinburgh 1982), 210–48.
6. Thorne, *House of Commons*, 520–2.
7. William Ferguson, *Scotland 1689 to the Present* (Edinburgh, 1994).
8. Dwyer and Murdoch, 'Paradigms and politics', 237.
9. William Ferguson, 'The Electoral System in the Scottish Counties before 1832', *Stair Society Miscellany 2* (1984), 261–94.
10. Bruce Lenman, *The Jacobite Risings in Britain 1689–1746* (London, 1980); Alistair and Henrietta Tayler, *Jacobites of Aberdeenshire and Banffshire in the Forty-Five* (Aberdeen, 1928).
11. Alistair and Henrietta Tayler, *A Jacobite Exile* (London, 1937).
12. Ibid., 211.
13. Alistair and Henrietta Tayler, *Lord Fife and his Factor: Being the Correspondence of James, Second Lord Fife 1729–1809* (London, 1925).

14. Michael Fry, *The Dundas Despotism* (Edinburgh, 1992).
15. This account is drawn from Thorne, *House of Commons,* 520–2.
16. Ibid., 520.
17. Ibid., 521.
18. Alistair and Henrietta Tayler, *The Book of the Duffs* (2 vols) (Edinburgh, 1914), 466–90.
19. Aberdeen University Special Libraries and Archives (hereafter AUSLA), Duff MS 3175/431, John Duff, Newton of Auchentoul to Fife in London, 26 January 1788.
20. Tayler and Tayler, *Duffs,* 477–8, 474.
21. G. J. Bryant, 'Scots in India in the Eighteenth Century', *Scottish Historical Review,* LXIV, 1 (1985), 22–41.
22. H. Strachey, *Narrative of the Mutiny of the Officers of the Army in Bengal, in the Year 1766* (London, 1773), 11.
23. Tayler and Tayler, *Duffs,* 480.
24. D. Hancock, "An undiscovered ocean of commerce laid open': India, wine and the emerging Atlantic economy, 1703–1813' in H. V. Bowen, M. Lincoln and N. Rigby, *The Worlds of the East India Company* (Woodbridge, 2002), 166.
25. Tayler and Tayler, *Duffs,* 478–9.
26. D. Johnston, 'The Duff genealogical papers of Alistair and Henrietta Tayler', *Northern Scotland,* 7/1 (1986) 61–70; AUSLA, Duff MS 3175/1003, George Hay, Rothimay to Lord Braco, 8 November 1756.
27. Tayler and Tayler, *Duffs,* 479.
28. H. Ward and W. Roberts, *Romney: A Biographical and Critical Essay with a Catalogue Raisonne of his Works,* 2 vols (London, 1904), Vol. 2, 47.
29. Anne Buddle with Pauline Rohatgi and Iain Gordon Brown, *The Tiger and the Thistle: Tipu Sultan and the Scots in India 1760–1800* (Edinburgh, 1999).
30. A. Dirom, *A Narrative of the Campaign in India which Terminated the War with Tippoo Sultan in 1792* (London, 1793), 112.
31. AUSLA, Duff MS 3175/408/1, List for 'Sir James Duff suppose him a Candidate' 1793.
32. Ibid., William Rose to Fife, Montcoffer, 28 August 1793.
33. Ibid.
34. Ibid., catalogue 2226/ 175/2, 21 April 1790, Alexander Gordon, Letterfourie to Rose.
35. Ibid., Duff MS 3175/408/2 Fife to Dundas, 20 March 1794.
36. National Archives of Scotland (hereafter NAS), High Court of Justiciary JC3/48, Minutes October 1796, defence information.
37. NAS, JC3/48, Minutes May 1796, prosecution information.
38. NAS, JC26/285, Proceedings 1796.
39. Ibid.
40. Ibid.
41. AUSLA, Duff MS 3175/268 George Stewart at Banff to Lord Fife, 5 November 1795; evidence of Fife at Duff House, 9 November 1795.
42. NAS, JC3/48.
43. Ibid.
44. AUSLA, Duff MS 3175/268, 7 December 1795, Fife from Edinburgh to Stewart Soutter and Alex Stronach; Stronach to Souter, 13 January 1796.
45. NAS, JC26/285, Disposition of Fyfe, at Keith to Peter Cameron, 4 December 1795.
46. NAS, JC26/285, Fyfe to Rose, 14 November 1786.
47. NAS, JC3/48, Fife to Rose 2 May 1787, emphasis in original.
48. NAS, JC26/285, Disposition of Fyfe, at Keith to Peter Cameron, 4 December 1795.

49. That Fyfe was not necessarily an altogether reliable witness is suggested by his involvement in another court case, which finished up on appeal to the House of Lords. In this Fyfe was found to have manipulated a dying man to write a new will in Fyfe's favour and then to have used the Procurator Fiscal for Banffshire to oppress the man's relations. The result was that the new will was quashed and Fyfe was required to pay damages. (T. Paton, *Reports of Cases Decided in the House of Lords upon Appeal from Scotland from 1753 to 1813*, Vol. 3 (Edinburgh 1853).)
50. Michael Davies, 'Prosecution and radical discourse during the 1790s: the case of the Scottish sedition trials', *International Journal of the Sociology of Law*, 33 (2005), 148–58.
51. NAS, JC3/48, information for Lieutenant Fyfe, May 1796.
52. Dwyer and Murdoch, 'Paradigms and politics', 235.
53. Ferguson, *Scotland*, 242.
54. Tayler and Tayler, *Fife and his factor*, 231.
55. Ibid., 237.
56. Ibid., 253.
57. Ibid., 18 June 1787, 190.
58. Ibid., 12 August 1765, 18.
59. Tayler and Tayler, *Duffs*, 479, 488.
60. Iain Gordon Brown, 'Griffins, Nabobs and a Seasoning of Curry Powder. Walter Scott and the Indian Theme in Life and Literature' in Anne Buddle with Pauline Rohatgi and Iain Gordon Brown, *The Tiger and the Thistle*; Edgar Johnson, *Sir Walter Scott: The Great Unknown*, Vol. 1 (New York, 1970).

SCOTS IN THE HUDSON'S BAY COMPANY, C. 1779–C. 1821

SUZANNE RIGG

Scotland's involvement with the Arctic fur trade, which can be traced back to 1683, twenty-four years before the Act of Union, was to persist for almost three centuries. As employees in the service of the Hudson's Bay Company (HBC), generation after generation of Scots migrated temporarily to the territory that now forms vast swathes of northern Canada. This English enterprise, established in 1670 by Prince Rupert and seventeen other gentlemen, was granted a royal charter by King Charles II. The group of merchants was awarded control of an area called Rupert's Land, which was defined as the lands drained by rivers flowing into Hudson's Bay, and amounted to a colossal territory, fifty times the size of Scotland. Within this domain, the governing gentlemen were permitted to establish laws, colonies and armies, but initially limited their sphere of activity to trade.

Few members of the London Committee, as the governing body of the HBC became known, ever set foot in Rupert's Land, but directed operations from the HBC's headquarters in London. They developed a practice whereby British personnel were contracted, typically for three to five years, and sent thousands of miles across the Atlantic to the shores of Hudson's Bay. The Company ships anchored at the southern end of this inland sea, at the mouths of the rivers draining into Hudson's Bay. Posts, also known as houses, forts and factories, were constructed on the nearby marshy landscape and soon came to include Moose, Churchill, York, Rupert, Albany, and Eastmain (see Figure 1).

Employees were stationed at these remote establishments, which were at least 100 miles apart, and had to adapt to working life in an extremely cold sub-arctic climate. They were organised hierarchically and generally categorised into two distinct groupings, 'gentlemen', sometimes called 'officers', and 'men', also known as 'servants'.[1] The former were entrusted with managing the business in Rupert's Land and served as intermediaries between the London Committee and the latter group, who formed the bulk of the workforce.

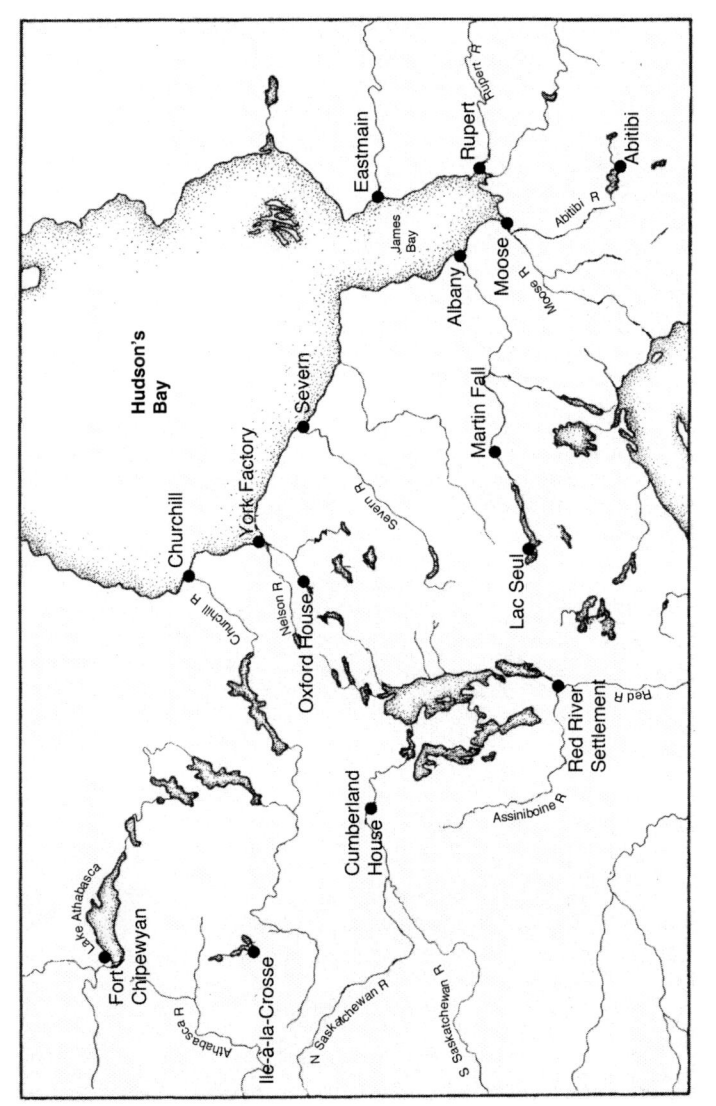

Figure 1. Hudson's Bay.

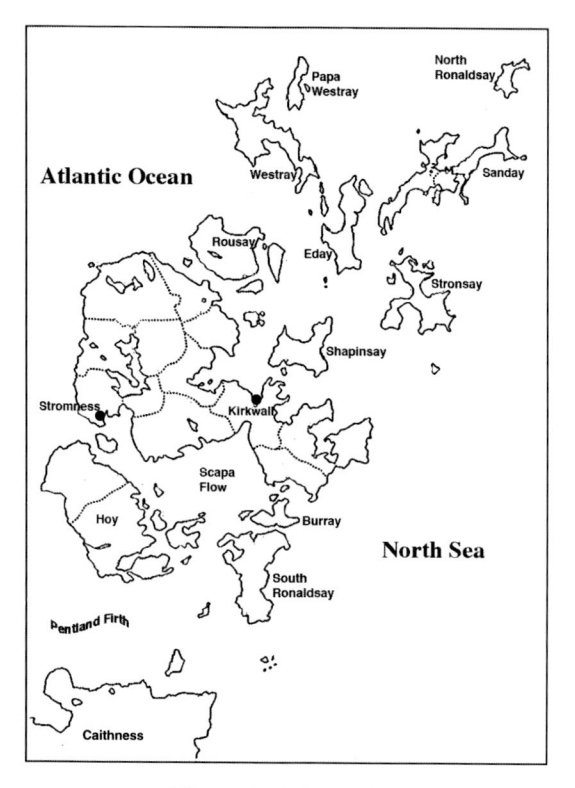

Figure 2. Orkney Isles.

For the first century of the Company's operations, which remained at Hudson's Bay, the personnel needs of the HBC were small. A recruitment ethos was established in which the directors prioritised the employment of English 'country lads' and Scots, largely due to their perceived qualities of subordination, sobriety, obedience and ability to endure deprivation.[2] The early recruitment practice of hiring a few Scots (from Leith) in the 1680s was given impetus by shortages of English manpower during the French–British conflict in the 1690s and the subsequent outbreak of the War of the Spanish Succession. Labour was recruited in the Orkney Islands (see Figure 2) when the Company ships made a final stop for supplies en route to Hudson's Bay and, as this practice continued, by the 1730s the employment of Orcadians had become firmly established.[3]

For these sojourners, the motivation was to make some money before eventually returning to better prospects at home. However, it came at the price of being separated from their families and enduring laborious work in a geographically remote and unforgiving environment. Working in temperatures as low as −50 degrees Fahrenheit, employees spent most of their time outdoors collecting firewood, hunting, and constructing or repairing trading posts. These posts were widely dispersed, occasioning the need for long, hazardous journeys on snow-covered ground or in canoes to secure food, medical, and trade supplies. Physical conditions were undoubtedly harsh and employees were often preoccupied with their own survival, but the primary purpose of their employment was to conduct the fur trading business.

Trading posts were manned by employees and stocked with European goods, including knives, axes, kettles and blankets. Members of the Cree, Chipewyan and Assiniboia tribes travelled down to Hudson's Bay in late spring to barter their furs and to act as middlemen, exchanging furs on behalf of distant tribes such as the Blackfoot. Beaver pelts were favoured by the HBC due to European demand for felt hats, but they also accepted marten, otter, fox, bear and wolf furs. When the seasonal trade was complete, the furs were sorted and packed by HBC employees ready for shipment to London. Two or three HBC vessels made an annual trip to Hudson's Bay, arriving in summer with new employees, trade goods and supplies, and departing in early autumn before they would be trapped by the onset of winter and the freezing over of Hudson's Bay. On the reverse journey the ships carried returning employees and consignments of furs, which were taken to London, where they were auctioned and made into fashionable apparel.

The HBC had developed a structured routine, which proved long-standing, but the Company's stability was often threatened by warfare and trading rivalries. Between 1686 and 1713 Britain's recurring conflict with France encroached upon operations in Hudson's Bay as French interlopers attacked and seized HBC posts. The Company's exclusive right to trade in Rupert's Land was also contested when French fur traders intercepted natives en route to trade at Hudson's Bay. Hostilities ceased in 1713 with the signing of the Treaty of Utrecht, when the French traders surrendered the posts and trade around Hudson's Bay.

The HBC re-established its posts, but at that juncture did not attempt to expand its activities further into its chartered territory. In 1749 this continuing inertia led to a damning critique in Britain when a former employee accused the Company of 'sleeping by the frozen sea'.[4] The stagnant operations of the HBC contrasted poorly with the vigorous initiatives shown by private French traders who crossed the continent towards the Rockies in the pursuit of quality furs. It was only following the British conquest of Canada in 1763, when British merchants began to move into the successful Montreal-based fur trade, that the HBC stirred, constructing its first inland post, Cumberland House, in 1774. Aside from being able to compete more effectively against rival traders, this also meant that the HBC's reliance on middlemen diminished, as its employees came into direct contact with the fur trappers. Pressure mounted to continue expansion when some of the Montreal-based merchants, many of whom were Scottish Highlanders, formally coalesced as the North West Company (NWC) in 1779. Employing skilled and experienced French Canadian *voyageurs* and injecting capital into the business, the new company immediately presented itself as a formidable rival.

The first century of the HBC's existence was long and difficult but the era after 1779 was a particularly critical one. The Company grappled with the new challenges presented by the expansion of commerce and settlements throughout Rupert's Land. Its route of expansion followed the river networks leading from Hudson's Bay along the Churchill, Nelson, Severn, Albany and Moose rivers, and eventually west to the Rockies on the Saskatchewan River, north on the Athabasca, and southwest to the Red River and Assiniboine River, near present-day Winnipeg, Manitoba. The labour force already had to adapt to life in the freezing tundra, and now also had to contend with long expeditions through wilderness terrain, as they tried to establish new relationships with native tribes and set up trading posts.

'Country skills', such as a familiarity with native languages and the ability to operate a canoe, became increasingly important assets for employees engaged in inland work.[5] Birchbark canoes were the main form of inland transport as they were fast, handled rapids well, and were light, making them easy to portage – carry overland – between bodies of water and around obstacles such as waterfalls. The main disadvantage of canoes was their fragility. A variety of other vessels, including those known as the Albany boats, Churchill boats, freight boats, and Red River boats, were also used on these inland expeditions as they had the advantage of pushing through ice and carrying more freight than canoes. However, they were difficult to portage and often had to be tracked, which involved towing the boat with a haul line. They did not come to replace the canoe as the main form of water transport until after 1821, when a uniform design was used, which later became known as the York boat.[6]

Apart from meeting the new demands of the developing inland fur trade, the HBC also faced an aggressive trading competition with the NWC. A feud developed between the two companies as they fought to win over new native trading partners, establishing posts side by side across the country, with the NWC approaching from the east, along the St Lawrence and Ottawa Rivers. These tensions were exacerbated by over-trapping, which decreased the availability of beaver supplies, eventually pushing the trade into the beaver-rich north west of the country. The rivalry only added to the HBC's problems as it increased the cost of furs at a time when the Company was already struggling financially, due to problems further afield in Europe.

The outbreak of the French revolutionary wars and later, the Napoleonic wars, created problems for the HBC, most notably labour shortages and financial difficulties. The value of the Company's stock fell, the market for furs faltered and the price of trade goods and provisions increased. With falling profits and mounting debt, the HBC reached a crisis point and, in 1810, finally addressed its problems, reorganising the London Committee and introducing proposals for retrenchment. Aside from trying to increase the efficiency of the Company, the HBC also sanctioned a colony in an area of Rupert's Land called Assiniboia. Thomas Douglas, the fifth earl of Selkirk, had purchased shares in the Company and in return fulfilled his ambition to found a settlement of Highlanders. It was not an entirely disinterested venture as it was intended that Selkirk would provide the HBC with labourers and provisions from the colony at Red River, and that retired HBC officers would eventually be granted allotments of land in the settlement.[7] The broader implications of the colony were huge, obstructing NWC trade routes, cutting off its food supplies, and displacing the offspring (known as the Métis) of its employees and native women who had settled in the area. The NWC believed that the settlement was a conspiracy to ravage its fur trade and therefore determined to oppose it to the full, supporting Métis attacks on the colony, which culminated in bloodshed in 1816 when at least twenty-two people were shot dead. This turbulent phase in HBC history drew to a close in 1821 when the two trading companies, suffering substantial human, material, and financial losses, were compelled to merge, resulting in a complete reorganisation of the trade.

Numerous scholars have remarked on the prominence of Scots in the HBC but only recently have Marjory Harper and T. M. Devine examined their involvement from a Scottish perspective. These studies consider Scottish participation in the fur trade in the broader context of diaspora and Empire, and are a useful addition to John Nicks' preliminary survey of a group of Orkneymen in the HBC during the forty years prior to its merger with the NWC.[8] Edith Burley's work is also helpful in bringing to light some neglected aspects of the working class experience as she focuses on the HBC as a business in the second century of the Company's operation.[9]

This article examines Scottish involvement in the HBC during the taxing period of 1779–1821, focusing on the ways in which Scots, and Orcadians in particular, became increasingly central to the Company's success. It also explores the enduring appeal of sojourning in Rupert's Land, surveying career prospects and mechanisms for advancement. Although Scots encountered opportunities for betterment in Rupert's Land, fur trade employment was certainly not unambiguously attractive and this study also investigates the challenges of working in an inhospitable environment. Finally, it delves into issues of identity and repatriation, looking at the impact of Scottish involvement in the fur trade on individuals, families and the home community.

Recruitment Policies and Practices

Scots had become an integral part of the HBC in the first hundred years of its existence, yet they did not truly monopolise the Company until after 1779 when inland expansion became the Company's priority. Successful expansion was dependent on increasing the workforce with 'most able and enterprizen Labourers' and Orkney seemed an ideal source due to its convenient location and the abundance of its labour supply.[10] Yet there was one crucial flaw in this plan: the HBC lacked an organised recruitment scheme, customised to meet the new demands of the inland trade. In the 1780s recruitment still rested in the hands of the ships' captains who simply selected workers at Stromness before voyaging to Hudson's Bay.[11]

The inadequacy of the HBC's method of staffing created several obstacles to expansion. Labour shortages became well known in Rupert's Land with deficiencies in the complement at Moose post restricting expansion to the newly established house at Abitibi, near the present day Ontario-Quebec border. Reports from York Factory also advocated a larger quota of men and canoes, but cautioned that this could not be done until 'more capable servants' were engaged.[12] This stemmed from a failure of the Committee members to consider whether the servants who had previously been suitable for the fur trade – obedient, hard working and content with low wages – would remain so in the new environment in which the Company operated. Servants on inland duty could spend as long as two months travelling in winter, covering as many as thirty miles a day, wearing snowshoes and hauling loaded sleds.[13] They had to acquire expertise in canoemanship in order to undertake long journeys on the network of waterways and were expected to exert themselves, often while suffering from hunger and fatigue. Many Orkneymen were found to be too old or too infirm to withstand the new rigours of the fur trade, and those who were able bodied were not always willing. One man would only go inland if bestowed with 'various presents', while an officer warned the managers that in order to build settlements they would be 'liable to some bribing'.[14]

The Company management realised that by relinquishing the responsibility of recruitment to the captains, they had little control over the composition and size of the labour force. Perhaps the assertion by Orcadian officer, William Tomison, in 1790, that there were many Orkneymen willing to enter the service and fifty more could have been procured if wanted, prompted them to react.[15] The Committee realised that in order to capitalise on this source of cheap labour, change was imperative. They took a significant step towards formalising the recruitment process in 1791, by hiring an agent, David Geddes, to be stationed permanently in Stromness.[16] The benefits of such organised recruitment were immediately apparent as the annual entry rate increased and Orcadians soon became more prominent in the Company, prompting the London Committee to comment that there are 'so many Cromarties Isbisters Spences... in the Company's Service'.[17]

However, imperial conflict had once again broken out between Britain and France, and competition for Orkney-based manpower began to hinder Geddes' recruitment efforts. Complaints of war-induced labour shortages proliferated in the HBC and the Company Secretary stated that 'there is no forcing Men to go against their will'.[18] Yet the London Committee found other ways through which the Company could secure a workforce. Financial inducements of one or two guineas were offered to new recruits, and the directors tried to retain existing servants in Hudson's Bay by warning them that they would 'be press'd into his majesty's service' if they returned home, later threatening that they would be forced to pay their own passage back across the Atlantic.[19] By the turn of the century these tactics appeared to have succeeded, as there was a substantial increase in the workforce and the HBC's settlements now extended more than a thousand miles into the interior.

Orcadian participation had risen almost two-fold since 1789, amounting to 418 men out of the entire 524 employees, but the recruitment scheme turned out to be a double-edged sword, as reliance on one source of labour left the Company vulnerable if that supply dried up.[20] It was paradoxical that while the HBC had been successfully increasing the Orcadian percentage of the workforce, locals had actually been turning against the enterprise in Orkney.[21] One parish minister echoed other opponents of emigration at that time, complaining that HBC employees were not defending their country. Critics emphasised the hazardous conditions in Hudson's Bay and the 'paltry sum of L.6', offered as a salary.[22] The effect of public denunciation of the Company by such influential parties was potentially damaging, and was further inflamed by negative representations circulated by returning servants. The murder of some HBC employees by the Inuit in 1794 seemed 'to operate very powerfully at the Orknies against Men engaging' and it was believed that it would 'require a little time to efface'.[23]

Discontented men found alternative outlets and although the army, navy and fisheries were options, engaging in the fur trade had actually opened up new avenues of employment for Orkneymen, namely, service with rival traders, the NWC. The Montreal-based company had travelled across the Rockies, reached the Pacific coast, and ventured north to the Arctic Ocean, but despite holding the lead in the trading competition, the NWC was not immune to the strains caused by expansion and competition, and it too struggled to obtain sufficient numbers of men.[24] There is some evidence to suggest that either due to labour shortages or as a tactic to gain advantage in the commercial competition, the NWC directors encroached upon the Orcadian labour supply. The Peace of Amiens had offered the HBC hopes of a respite from labour shortages, but these were quashed when the NWC engaged forty to fifty Orcadians, 'most of whom were the Company's late servants'.[25]

Faced with the devastating effects of negative opinion and a fierce competition for manpower, the HBC directors were compelled to broaden their recruitment sphere and establish new sources of Scottish labour. Recruiting agents focused on the Highlands and Shetland and in 1805 the *King George III* was ordered to stop in Lerwick to 'take on board all such Men as may have been engaged ...' before proceeding to Orkney.[26] Non-Orcadian Scottish participation increased with these recruiting efforts, but they still comprised less than 3 per cent of servants in 1812: Orkneymen continued to make up the bulk of the workforce. The Company had overlooked their rumour-mongering in the early years of the decade, and continued to seek and encourage their employment, luring them into the HBC with monetary awards.[27]

Financial and coercive measures, along with attempts to extend recruitment to other parts of Scotland, ensured the survival of the enterprise, but such approaches could not be continued indefinitely as the business was in serious financial difficulties. The lengthy war with France meant that trade goods were increasingly expensive and there was not only a decline in the market for fur, but the export of furs to Europe had been stopped. The HBC attempted to surmount its problems in 1810 by a reorganisation of the business, known as the 'New System'. This strategy was designed to improve efficiency and included the recruitment of servants equipped to contend with the intensification of rivalry with the NWC.[28]

As the trading contest raged between the companies in the early nineteenth century employees became increasingly embroiled in violent altercations. Beaver shortages had forced the trade north-westwards towards an area called the Athabasca, around Lake Athabasca, where good quality furs were abundant. On this frontier, opposition was particularly strong as the NWC conducted campaigns of harassment, pressurising the HBC to vacate the area.[29] Whereas earlier HBC concerns had centred on the problem of an inadequate supply of labour, its main objective was now to tackle the long-standing inefficiency of its workforce.

Colin Robertson, a Scotsman who had previously been in the employ of the HBC's rivals, now offered the Company his advice. He noted that the NWC's energetic, subservient workforce was an advantage, whereas the HBC's labourforce was a major stumbling block, consisting of a supply of men 'very ill calculated for the country', including boys, old men and 'lunatics'.[30] Compliance, subordination and a positive work ethic continued to be displaced by complacency and intransigence, Colin Robertson observing that when 'Orkneymen were either discontented with the post or their Master, you can never get them to do their duty but by halves' and 'if the place they are ordered to has only the name of being hard, or the voyage difficult to perform, they will throw a hundred obstacles in the way'.[31] The directors did not consider this obduracy as an 'intrinsic defect in the character of the Orkney men', but attributed it to mismanagement, which partially explains why Orcadians had continued to be the mainstay of recruitment despite similar evidence of insubordination twenty years earlier.[32] The environment of the fur trade was changing however, and in the new climate of hostile rivalry the Orcadian tendency to negotiate and bargain over duties, wages and orders became of paramount concern to the Committee.[33] Instead of countering Orcadian misbehaviour, the management strove to introduce new employees who were not characterised by such waywardness, and so a decade of experimentation ensued.

The search for energetic, obedient and driven servants to form a vigorous opposition against the Nor'westers again broadened the recruitment sphere throughout Scotland, introducing more Highlanders, Lowlanders and Western Islanders to the Company, as well as Canadians and other Europeans. For the first time in the HBC's history, men from Inverness-shire and Ross-shire peppered the list of personnel; at Edmonton alone there were over forty men from Lewis and Inverness. Within a few years, virtually no part of Scotland was untouched by the HBC, as men from Glasgow, Elgin, Lanark, Edinburgh, Blair Atholl, Reay, and Dumfries joined the Company.[34]

These new recruitment strategies posed a threat to the continued prominence of Orkneymen. Exemplary men were still a rare find in Orkney and 'Mr Geddes' bad bargains' continued to arrive, but the introduction of men from other regions showed that everyone had failings.[35] The Glaswegians and Irish were considered mutinous, the 'Inverness men' were prone to debt, and many other recruits were considered unfit.[36] The realisation that other workers also had their flaws, coupled with Orcadian experience in the inland trade and their continued cheapness, reinforced the Company's belief that Orkneymen were an asset.

There were actually clear signs that the directors still viewed Orcadians as their core workforce: a prospective recruit from Yorkshire had petitioned the Company for employment in 1815 but was advised that it 'is supplied with servants from the Orkney Islands'.[37] In fact, the new recruitment practices appear to have had only a small effect on Orcadian participation in the HBC. Orkney contributed a total of 290 men to the Company's workforce in 1812, which represented two-thirds of the payroll at the time. This was not early enough to see any effects of the 'New System', but by 1816 Orcadian participation had decreased to 266 men. Although they had barely dropped in absolute numbers, they had fallen quite considerably as a proportion of the Company's employees, making up just over 50 per cent of the workforce. Thereafter their involvement actually rose: by 1819 there were 319 Orkneymen in the service, constituting 51 per cent of the workforce, and this trend looked set to continue.[38]

The perceived loyalty of Orcadians seems to have been another of their redeeming factors. Although the Committee had reservations about their fidelity during the labour shortages in the early years of the French wars, Orkneymen had served well in meeting quotas and acting as a fallback under the 'New System' when recruitment faltered elsewhere. For instance, when recruiting agents were unable to meet a small quota from Inverness in 1820, Orkney was able to provide a surplus.[39] The directors declined to engage any men from the Highlands the following year, and instead looked to Lewis and Orkney to provide the required quantity of recruits.[40] Thus, when the fur trade rivalry ended in 1821, Orkneymen were again the mainstay of recruitment, with the assistance of men from Lewis.[41] The Company vessels were routed first via Stromness, and then by Stornoway, before proceeding to Hudson's Bay.

Arctic Opportunity: Constructing a Career in the HBC

Just as Orkneymen were of vital and persistent significance to the HBC, so the fur trade offered a crucial lifeline and avenue to betterment for many Orcadians. Domestic prospects such as agriculture, fishing, and manufacturing were limited, fruitless, or undeveloped in Orkney during the late eighteenth century, and endemic hardships were periodically exacerbated by famine.[42] A versatile temporary migratory tradition meant that members of Orcadian society who laboured under crippling poverty, as well as those who were moderately comfortable and simply sought to improve their lot, had access to numerous opportunities for improvement.[43]

The decision to enter the service of the HBC in particular appears to have been a rational one, based on the prospect of fixed wages and stable long-term employment, attractions which were promoted by recruiting agents and advertised on handbills in Orkney.[44] Basic utilities such as accommodation were provided, heightening anticipation that 'in Hudson's Bay you may nearly save the Whole of your Wages yearly'.[45] The 'fair prospect of providing for the future & guarding against the consequences of Poverty' was probably sweetened further by the offer of an advance on their wages when they engaged.[46] This beckoning of financial betterment was bolstered by the knowledge that family and friends would also be working in remote Rupert's Land.

One further appeal lay in the considerable scope for advancement. Although most employees entered the HBC in low-ranking positions such as unskilled labourers, any servant who wished to achieve a higher status within the Company and was willing to learn new 'country' skills, could usually realise his ambition.[47] When the fur trade spread inland, employees had the opportunity to advance through the development of canoe skills.[48] Some were reluctant to go inland, but others were willing to master the manoeuvres and navigation of canoes upon the often-turbulent rivers, and in consequence, many labourers progressed to the station of 'canoeman' by the end of their first contract. These positions were synonymous in rank and salary, but canoemen had better career prospects. Once employees had grasped the rudiments, they were promoted to the second tier of proficiency as bowmen, and thereafter to the station of steersman.[49]

Ambitious employees who wished to improve their prospects beyond the confines of hard physical labour really needed to acquire trading skills such as thorough knowledge of a native tribe and its language and customs. In fact the directors considered employees to be 'of little use' until they acquired such experience and for this reason servants usually engaged for a term of five years, some of which might be spent living with a native tribe.[50] During these residencies, employees endeavoured to build a good rapport with native traders, master indigenous skills such as hunting and trapping, and learn the tribe's language. Despite a common distaste for the tribal lifestyle, Scots demonstrated a flair for learning indigenous languages and Orcadian Magnus Spence, who entered the Company as a labourer in 1783, soon became adept in country skills, triggering his promotion to steersman and linguist in the 1790s.[51]

Some employees successfully infiltrated the upper ranks of the HBC through their skills and experience in the field, whereas others already possessed the virtues sought in officers when they initially entered the service. The widely dispersed structure of the HBC meant that the London Committee required officers to write details on all operations in Rupert's Land in order to manage the Company effectively. Literacy and education were valuable assets and educated men, who often entered the service as writers (clerks), had remarkably good prospects for advancement. The upward mobility of these young writers tended to be rapid, as in the case of James Russell from Shapinsay, who rose to the position of district master only seven years after his entry as a writer in 1807.[52]

The Company even appreciated a basic literacy in its employees as the ongoing establishment of inland houses generated an urgent need for additional masters. Inland posts were often small, requiring minimal administration, and so the Company endorsed the appointment of less well educated, but literate men, to these stations.[53] Orcadian James Tait entered the service as a labourer in 1778 and demonstrated his literacy when he maintained journals at Manchester House, near the North Saskatchewan River. He was left 'in charge' of the post in 1790, being 'the properest person and the most steady', and subsequently served as master and trader until his return to Orkney in 1812.[54]

Country skills and literacy undoubtedly facilitated the upward mobility of men in the HBC, but ethnic-based patronage also proved useful. Scottish servants in the Company had prior bonds, which they imported into the fur trade and employed to expedite overseas advancement. Orcadian webs were of practical utility and although the vertical structure of the HBC, and the infrastructure of Rupert's Land, meant that Orcadian coteries and networks were not blatantly visible, their subtle operation could be detected within the Scots' endeavours for advancement.

Most recruits entered the service in low-ranking positions, but some Orcadians with connections in the Company, whether family, friends, or the recruiting agent, gained access to hard-to-obtain positions. Alexander Kennedy's career break emerged out of the patronage of a senior Orcadian officer in the HBC. Kennedy was selected as a writer in 1798, under the auspices of John Ballenden, and it was hoped that 'he may do credit' to the recommendation.[55] The advancement of James Kirkness also seems to have been fostered by the patronage of a fellow Orcadian. Chief factor, William Sinclair, originated from Kirkness' home parish, Harray in Orkney, and in 1812, Kirkness worked under Sinclair's command in the Winnipeg District. These men would have shared social and working lives as well as a connection based on a common local origin. Kirkness clearly benefited from these circumstances as Sinclair recommended him to the Company directors and increased his wages from £25 to £40 a year, a sum of which he was 'highly deserving'. The bond between the men was cemented when Kirkness married Sinclair's mixed-blood daughter, Jane. It is probable that the support of a chief factor assisted in Kirkness' ongoing advancement, which culminated in promotion to the station of district master in 1818.[56] But although Scottish patronage was a constructive mechanism for advancement to those who could obtain it, and recommendations, salary increases, and occasionally promotions materialised out of Orcadian networks, it was not essential to career success.

Following the reorganisation of the HBC in 1810, most opportunities for advancement were curtailed and few low-ranking Orkneymen were newly appointed into the high ranks. An influx of educated Scots (from the mainland) into managerial positions had to some extent lessened the Orcadians' opportunities for promotion. Education and social status became increasingly important, and the implementation of patronage was restricted as the governors were instructed to appoint 'to the situation of traders such Men only as are properly qualified for conducting the business'.[57] Uneducated men who had risen from the low ranks discovered new limitations to their aspirations and, for instance, John Robertson, who rose from the status of labourer to become outpost master at Nelson River, was regarded in 1814 as 'not qualified for a higher station'.[58]

However, some of the senior officers in the Company supported internal recruitment practices and opposed the new strategies, which conflicted with the needs of the trade in Rupert's Land. Scottish officer William Auld complained about the inexperience of the new, externally appointed officers, who lacked an understanding of trade, native tribes and customs.[59] Senior personnel highlighted the ways in which enterprising employees, who did not fit the directors' description of the ideal officer, compensated for their supposed shortcomings. The high value placed on experience in the field meant that some Orkneymen continued to rise within the Company, despite their apparent lack of officer quality.[60] According to Company policy, Orcadian James Slater was ill equipped for his position as outpost master at Osnaburgh as he was illiterate and had insufficient authority over his subordinates. Yet, he offset this apparent deficiency by his trading skills and his aggregate trade return was such that senior officers believed it 'counterpoises his want of education'. It earned him the respect of his colleagues in the officer rank and by 1818 he had been promoted to a district master, being 'an Officer of much merit'.[61]

Some employees may have failed to ascend the occupational ladder as far as they had hoped, particularly after 1810, but the earning potential that was available throughout the ranks meant that unskilled men still found profit in low-ranking service. The occupational hierarchy was not always reflected in salary and it seems that longevity of service and apparent fidelity were actually held in higher regard than ability. In 1800, long-term unskilled labourer Thomas Miller earned £25–£30, when fellow Orcadian Andrew Moar, an officer and master of Neoskweskau, on the Eastmain River, earned the same amount.[62]

Employees also received wage increases that were often far greater than the Company had intended. Officers frequently deviated from the customary wage policy, and amended salaries on the ground, in response to practical needs. Labourer Magnus Flett served one five-year contract at £8 and then stated that he wished to return home in 1802. This may have been an example of servants' 'mere Tricking' when, aware of labour shortages, they threatened to return home only in order to receive better earnings. Under pressure to retain hands, superiors often conceded, and in Flett's case, persuaded him to continue in the service for a second contract, at the elevated rate of £25 per annum.[63] Thus, a sojourn in Rupert's Land provided the avenue to improvement that most men sought, but temporary migratory employment in the Hudson's Bay Company was still a gamble; the environment in which sojourners sought to better their fortunes presented as many risks to their welfare, as it did opportunities for advancement.

Life in the Fur Trade

The perils that accompanied work in the fur trade were considerable and were perhaps at their worst during the 'long, gloomy, and most severe winter' experienced in Rupert's Land.[64] John McDonald, the Inverness agent, reported in 1819 that many young Scots had returned home prematurely after being disabled by frostbite.[65] Winter expeditions were, of course, most dangerous, as John Malcolm from Walls in Orkney discovered when he became disorientated and subsequently frozen at Gloucester Lake, near Martin Fall, in 1817. He was sent for surgical assistance and had 'the misfortune to lose both his Feet'.[66] Malcolm was actually fortunate not to perish, as prolonged exposure to the elements was a common cause of death.[67] In that same year, James Clouston from Stenness accidentally became separated from his companions while travelling through snow in the Albany District and perished after spending the night alone with 'neither Hatchet flint or Stick, to make a fire'.[68]

Servants' ability to undertake work in an inhospitable climate was further weakened by their inadequate diet. When the Company moved inland, men were increasingly reduced to 'a deplorable state of starvation'.[69] Employees' levels of vulnerability depended on their degree of isolation, and their ease of communication with the outside world. Bayside posts were usually well provided with imported goods, including pork, beef, flour, oatmeal and barley, but even they had to rely upon natural resources to some degree, and it was feared at Eastmain in 1809 that 'the stock of European Meat will be consumed before the Spring supplies of Geese are received here'.[70]

Inland travellers and the inhabitants of isolated settlements rarely had much recourse to European provisions and relied on a precarious supply of local and seasonal produce such as fish, geese, partridges, rabbits, buffalo, and venison.[71] The nourishment of inland post employees largely depended on their access to such victuals, which often hinged on encountering and co-operating with the natives, who traded food in exchange for brandy, ammunition and tobacco.[72] The HBC's dependence on native contributions was pronounced, and one officer at Red Lake, near Lac Seul, observed in 1790 that 'we shall starve if the Natives does not supply us' with food.[73] It seems that employees developed an over-reliance on their contributions, and that this perhaps discouraged self-sufficiency. For instance, in 1800 a group of servants spent some time living off the provisions that they had traded from a native, as they had not yet made an effort to construct nets to catch their own fish.[74]

It was often no easy feat to supplement the Company rations as endeavours to fish and hunt were tempered by seasonal and environmental constraints. Although fishing became the chief sustenance for many posts, due to the abundance of rivers and the year-round sustainability resulting from the practice of ice fishing in winter, the same area could vary enormously in the availability of resources throughout each season and each year.[75] In 1800–1, the servants at Chipewyan Lake in the Athabasca managed to subsist on the returns of pike and suckers until March, when 'Fish being so very few and no prospect of getting any provisions from Indians', two men were sent to Nelson House as 'we are too many at this place'.[76]

Removal to a more prosperous location was not always possible due to the deplorable state of starvation under which some traders already laboured. In such cases, the servants could be pushed to radical measures to ensure survival, and it was not unusual to eat dogs or animal skins in the fur trade, when necessary.[77] Encumbering posts with extra mouths to feed could also bring whole settlements to the brink of starvation, as Albany experienced in 1816 when two Company ships were detained throughout the winter. The complement had to support thirty-one returned passengers whose arrival was an 'unexpected and unpleasant sight'.[78] The heavy dependence on meagre rations caused malnutrition and mortality: Chief factor William Sinclair lost one of his men to fatigue and hunger that year; another two almost shared the same fate, and many others contended with scurvy. This was not an isolated incident as thirteen sailors lost their lives to starvation and scurvy during the previous year when the ships had also been detained.[79]

The Committee's lack of foresight in provisioning the posts adequately in anticipation of such disasters only exacerbated the problem. Their inexperience of basic wilderness survival may have led them to overrate the natural food returns of the country, as well as employees' accessibility to, and skill in procuring, such country provisions. Unfortunately, the time-lag in communication meant that the management in London would not hear of the problems that were experienced until after the following year's supply of provisions had been shipped.

Yet the most common cause of death and injury in the HBC was work-related accidents. In the early 1800s, George Gladman, the Chief of Moose Fort, reported that 'we have had few instances of sickness, but accidents have deprived us of the services of some of the most useful hands'.[80] The *Statistical Account* for St Andrews and Deerness confirmed that some Orkneymen in the HBC were 'cut off by accidents every year'.[81] Drowning certainly became a common occurrence when the Company expanded and inexperienced employees had to venture into uncharted regions by canoe: by 1788 the directors were sending instructions to the Bay for 'recovering drowned people'.[82] It is not surprising that disproportionately high incidences of drowning afflicted Orkneymen during this period, as they tended to monopolise canoe-related stations.[83] Even those who were trained in the management of a canoe and had years of experience were not immune to the ordeals caused by rapids or exceptionally high waters. John Sinclair, whose position of steersman indicated that he must have been a proficient canoeman, met his end 'tumbling overboard' while attempting to settle a place near Eastmain in 1793.[84]

The London Committee was sympathetic to such misfortunes – occasionally providing financial compensation to needy family members – but equally, placed strict emphasis on the need for prudence. Some accidents did result from carelessness, particularly when handling firearms. Two fatalities in the 1790s were the consequence of accidental gunshots. One servant, G. Sinclair, was 'shot by another accidentally snapping a Gun and not knowing it was loaded the contents lodged in his Breast and he expired immediately', while James Scott was also shot by his companion in the thigh 'in a most shocking manner'.[85]

Reckless behaviour was occasionally fuelled by inebriation. The Company directors officially encouraged sobriety but as well as being a trading currency in the fur trade, alcohol was utilised for recreational purposes. Although alcoholism itself rarely caused mortality, heavy drinking was at the root of some deaths among fur traders.[86] The combination of alcohol and a severe climate proved lethal for one Orcadian servant, James Slater, who 'sat on the [frozen] River & got intoxicated' on rum with a fellow servant in 1816. His companion crawled back to headquarters but was 'unfit to give any intelligence concerning Slater, so that he lay all Night among the overflowings in the River'. When Slater was found on the ice the following morning, his exposed hands were frozen, and he died from his injuries three months later.[87]

It is difficult to gauge how many employees actually consumed to excess, or were addicted to alcohol. There are signs that a large part of the workforce was, if not dependent on, at least preoccupied with alcohol, as many had to be bribed by drink before they would work. Although excessive drinking, like any other debilitating habit or condition, threatened the maintenance of proper authority and discipline, as well as successful trade, the Company often seemed to pay only lip service to the need to regulate drinking. It is possible that the inefficiency, morbidity and mortality which resulted from inebriation, were perhaps cancelled out by the perception that alcohol was a necessary compensation and anaesthetic for the harshness of the working environment.

Issues of Identity and Repatriation

Conditions in the fur trade were undoubtedly challenging, but employees did not intend to settle in Rupert's Land on a permanent basis. The stimulus to migrate had been economic in nature and most servants aimed to make their money and return home as soon as was feasible. Many had the explicit intention of making money to support their families in Orkney during their absence. Individual obligations varied according to the personal make-up of each employee's family, but one officer commented in the 1790s that the 'chief part of your honours Servants have families often left destitute'.[88] These impoverished men entered the service in order to support their dependents, including wives, children and elderly parents.[89] Yet crippling poverty and family support were not the sole incentives to serve in the HBC; many servants also hoped to fulfil their own personal aspirations upon their return to Scotland.

Since the location in which they plied their trade and earned that money was so far from home, mechanisms had to be set in place to ensure that wages and savings were successfully repatriated to Scotland. To this end, a regulated system of remittances was instituted in the 1780s. All transactions in Rupert's Land were to be conducted on a credit/debit system. Employees could take up goods such as clothes, paper, soap, alcohol and tobacco from the posts and also order sums of money to people and financial institutions in Britain, without handling any cash directly. Liaison agents such as David Geddes were then appointed to arrange the payment of wages due to returners, in cash, in Orkney, and also the support money directed to employees' relatives. The Orcadian servants were reportedly 'very thankful' for this method of assisting their families.[90]

The administrators also implemented some guidelines to support their servants in the management of their accounts. Employees were not allowed to spend more than two thirds of their annual salary on goods and money orders.[91] They emphasised that these limitations were not designed to prevent men from 'furnishing themselves with comfortable Cloathing, or from assisting their Families at home' but 'originates in our attention to the Welfare of our Servants by curbing extravagance, and providing that they may not be exposed to Poverty and evil Courses when they come over'.[92]

The directors were perhaps aware that the Scots' encounter with the fur trade constituted far more than contractual participation in a commercial enterprise. It was also characterised by a complex set of social and cultural circumstances. Employees were separated from their families in an isolated environment, and partook in work that encouraged immersion in a new way of life. Entrenchment in the fur trade had the potential to relegate commitments in Scotland, or even modify servants' original objectives, leading to the neglect of those dependent on their support at home.

Recreational activities in Rupert's Land were an important antidote to the isolation and hardship of service, but excessive indulgence in pastimes like gambling and alcohol consumption resulted in debt to the HBC. Despite the Company's best efforts to prevent indebtedness by restricting expenditure and directing its chief factors to inspect all servants' bills to 'prevent Gaming & Extravagance', many employees ignored the rules and drew unapproved money orders. Overdrawn servants would not have their bills honoured and in 1810 at least twenty-six employees did not have their remittances complied with in Orkney, in consequence of their inadequate funds.[93]

Other families were not afforded any financial assistance because their sons or spouses had failed to leave an order to this effect with the HBC. In 1787, William Longmoor was notified that he would not receive his customary support money of £6, because his son Robert had forgotten to draft an assignment.[94] In such cases the Committee assumed that it was an oversight and informed the servant that a family member had been anticipating money. However, some employees simply did not want anyone to receive a payment on their account. The wife of employee David Sanderson persistently badgered the Company for money from his account from 1794 onwards, until the directors eventually demanded that the Orkney agent furnish her with £10 to 'stop her mouth & prevent her presenting the Committee with her letters'. They suggested that she apply to her spouse for an annual bill, but this seemingly was not sanctioned. In 1802 the directors wrote to Sanderson stressing that he ought to provide for his family and to acquaint them with the amount he would allow for subsistence. Under pressure, Sanderson did grant support money, but his wife went on to draw bills that exceeded the limit prescribed by her husband.[95]

Fractured relationships such as the Sandersons may have been an incentive to enter the Company, but equally, a reluctance to meet responsibilities in their home societies may have been due to the formation of competing commitments during a sojourn. British women were forbidden from voyaging to Rupert's Land, so in response to the segregated lifestyle in the Arctic, and the trading needs of both the Company and native tribes, new social customs had emerged in the fur trade. Many tribes were as eager as the Company managers to form and fortify partnerships, and one common means of doing so was to offer women to employees, temporarily or permanently, as a gesture of goodwill. These alliances clearly benefited employees as they provided sexual gratification and could ease the pressures of subsistence living, since native women served well as guides, hunters and interpreters. In turn, native women and their tribes sought economic rewards, including European goods and favourable trade.[96]

Although one observer later commented that the 'Scotchmen or Orkneymen who were in the Hudson Bay service... consorted with Cree women, sometimes giving them marriage and sometimes not', many of these relationships did develop into genuine attachments.[97] However, as the men were itinerants and native women were not permitted to return to Britain, a separation was inevitable.[98] Until the institution of the Red River colony, abandonment was a real possibility that all native partners faced, but the settlement eventually altered the course of some fur trade alliances as employees had the option of remaining in the colony with their country wives and mixed-blood offspring. In 1818 the Company was pleased to note that its servants 'consider the settlement of this Country so desirable an object'.[99] Although temporary migration was their intention, for a minority of employees the formation of family ties in Rupert's Land replaced taking a wife and mother from Britain, and permanent emigration became the inadvertent outcome of employment in the fur trade.[100]

The formation of 'mixed-blood' families in Rupert's Land or simply a lengthy absence may have severed some employees' ties with their homelands, but most retained close attachments to home. The HBC facilitated contact between servants and their Scottish families, permitting the exchange of letters and packages via the Company vessels, and these interchanges, along with informal communication networks among the Orcadian contingent, enabled employees to preserve their interest in family, community and local affairs.[101] For the most part employees remained mindful of their relatives and friends in Scotland and successfully repatriated the profits of the fur trade, bolstering private domestic economies.

Many remittances were regular orders and of such an amount that they could have constituted a vital portion of the household income, easing the outlay of rent, and the support of dependents. For instance, in the early 1800s, William Irvine, a labourer from Stromness, released funds varying from £5 5s to £6 6s, to his wife in Orkney, on an annual basis.[102] Some household economies were not wholly reliant on the earnings provided by HBC service and in such cases remittances could serve as an irregular top-up for family income or to ease the burden of unexpected domestic expenses. For instance, Oman Norquoy was able to bear the cost on behalf of his family for his mother's funeral expenses, remitting £4 to his sister for this purpose in 1814.[103] Employees who remitted in this manner were mindful of the economic difficulties that family members could endure in their absence, but their own aspirations for personal betterment were often the driving force behind their sojourn.

To this end, many servants sent large portions of their salaries to financial institutions such as Sir William Forbes' bank in Scotland, and the Bank of England. The directors boasted that 'there are very few, if any of the Company's Orkney Servants, after their first Contract is expired, who are not in the Habit of accumulating the fruits of their Industry & placing it in the public funds of the Bank of England'.[104] Although this was an embroidered statement, many employees did accrue capital, and some purchased annuities in the 3 per cent consolidated funds of the Bank of England. James Banks, an Orcadian labourer, invested in the funds in both 1792 and 1793, culminating in £255 of property, while Orcadian officer John Ballenden held £2,100 in 1798.[105]

The returns of the fur trade were rarely vast, particularly when compared to the fortunes reaped in the Chesapeake tobacco colonies, Caribbean sugar plantations, and India, but the proceeds were often sufficient to enable employees to obtain a hold on land at home. In the late eighteenth century, this generally took the form of renting farms, but in the early nineteenth century, a growing number of returners aspired to land ownership. Instead of entering fleeting tenancies, they used their returns to climb the social ladder and enter the property market.[106] John Brough served as a labourer in the HBC before acquiring landed property in Rendall in 1818. Others such as William Sinclair from Harray, who was Chief at Oxford House, between Lac Seul and Martin Fall, planned his future permanent homecoming while on furlough from service in 1814–15. He became the landholder of Eastquoy and Meadow in Harray, and subsequently returned to Hudson's Bay. Unfortunately the hazards of the fur trade meant that he did not live to enjoy the fruits of his hard work, as less than three years later he died at York factory.[107] Perhaps the only consolation in such misfortune was that these gains were often transferred to relatives.

Arctic employment yielded modest but significant rewards to Orkneymen and their families, and some fur traders ensured that these gains had a far-reaching impact by ploughing their profits into the wider society of Orkney. Several applied their savings to the maintenance or establishment of educational institutions, and the provision of poor relief in their local parishes in the islands. During thirty years of service, Orcadian Magnus Twatt accumulated funds in Sir William Forbes' bank in Edinburgh, and in 1796 bequeathed £700 of this money for schooling in his home town of Kirbister in Orphir. Following his death in Rupert's Land in 1801, the sum of money was laid out on landed security, while the interest was used to cover the costs of a school and a schoolmaster to teach the children in the parish of Orphir. Any surplus money was to be distributed annually to the poor in the same parish.[108]

Conclusion

Both Orcadians, and Scots more generally, gained and retained a remarkable foothold within the HBC, with the Orkney isles continuing to provide not only the fall-back labour supply, but also the crux of the recruitment effort, right up until the merger with the North West Company in 1821. Considering that the challenges posed by inland residence had served to deconstruct the management's long held stereotype of Orkneymen as submissive, obedient and tractable, it is even more remarkable that the HBC's dependence on Orkney endured. The perceived foibles of unfitness and insubordination were attributed to shoddy recruiting by the agents and mismanagement in Hudson's Bay. Moreover, the introduction of men from other localities showed that everyone had shortcomings. In fact, juxtaposed with other servants, the cheapness, convenience, perceived loyalty, and experience of Orkneymen rendered them invaluable to the concern.

The opportunities provided by inland expansion and the high value placed on the 'country skills' in which Orkneymen excelled meant that uneducated and unskilled men were not debarred from advancement. Yet the success of employees who worked in unskilled labouring positions, suggests that the terms in which advancement is viewed ought to be reconsidered, as some Orkneymen of a lowly occupational status successfully utilised their service with the HBC to acquire funded or landed property in Britain. It is probable that the return of such men who demonstrated the realistic outcomes that service could provide – sustaining domestic households, and safeguarding their own future through investment in stock or land – was the most persuasive factor in recruitment. Although the hardships of service did on occasion discourage men from continuing in, or re-engaging with the Company, illness and mortality were generally acceptable risks in imperial sojourning, and it is probable that most servants, having weighed up the hazards of service against the ensuing financial reward, found that employment in the fur trade remained worthwhile.

Notes

1. Michael Payne, *'The Most Respectable Place In the Territory': Everyday Life in Hudson's Bay Company Service York Factory, 1788–1870*, Studies in Archaeology, Architecture and History, National Historic Parks and Sites, Canadian Parks Service, Environment Canada (Ottawa, 1989), 28.
2. E. E. Rich (ed.), *Minutes of the Hudson's Bay Company 1679–1684: First Part 1679–1682* (Toronto, 1945), 251–77.
3. K. G. Davies (ed.), *Letters from Hudson Bay 1703–1740* (London, 1965), 22–3, 116, 129, 162, 165, 184–5, 199, 214; Rich, *The History of the Hudson's Bay Company, 1670–1870*, vol. 1 (London, 1958), 499; *The Statistical Account of Scotland* [hereafter *OSA*], vol. XX, St Andrews and Deerness, 265; National Archives of Scotland [hereafter NAS], RH15/14/41, Thomas Bannatyne, Charlton Island, to Anna Bannatyne, 1684.
4. Richard Glover, 'The Difficulties Of The Hudson's Bay Company's Penetration Of The West', *Canadian Historical Review*, 29: 3 (September 1948), 240.
5. Jennifer S. H. Brown, *Strangers In Blood: Fur Trade Company Families in Indian Country* (Vancouver, 1985), 28.
6. Dennis F. Johnson, *York boats of the Hudson's Bay Company: Canada's Inland Armada* (Calgary, 2006), 3, 19, 27, 30, 39.
7. J. M. Bumsted, 'The Affair at Stornoway, 1811', *The Beaver* (Spring, 1982), 53–4.
8. T. M. Devine, *Scotland's Empire, 1600–1815* (London, 2003); Marjory Harper, *Adventurers and Exiles: The Great Scottish Exodus* (London, 2004); John Nicks, 'Orkneymen in the Hudson's Bay Company, 1780–1821', in Carol M. Judd and Arthur J. Ray (eds), *Old Trails and New Directions: Papers of the Third North American Fur Trade Conference* (Toronto, 1980). See also Lucille H. Campey, *The Silver Chief. Lord Selkirk and the Scottish Pioneers of Belfast, Baldoon and Red River* (Toronto, 2003).
9. Edith I. Burley, *Servants of the Honourable Company: Work, Discipline and Conflict in the Hudson's Bay Company, 1770–1879* (Oxford, 1997).
10. Hudson's Bay Company Archives [hereafter HBCA], A.6/13, fos 73–76, 156d.
11. Ibid., A.5/2, fos 61, 120.
12. Ibid., A.11/45, fo. 157; B.121/a/4, fo. 45d; A.11/117, fos 21d–22, 59d.
13. Richard Glover (ed.), *David Thompson's Narrative, 1784–1812* (Toronto, 1962), 9.
14. HBCA, A.30/4, fos 15, 21–22; A.11/117, fos 21d–22, 126d; B.59/b/10, fos 3d–4; B.121/a/4, fo. 17d; A.30/2, fo. 21; A.5/2, fo. 50d; A.6/13, fo. 39d–40; B.121/a/4, fo. 17d; Burley, *Servants*, 74.
15. HBCA, A.11/117, fo. 56d.
16. Ibid., A.5/3, fos 54d, 57d.
17. Ibid., A.5/3, fos 69, 73, 80d, 95d, 100d.

18. Ibid., B.135/a/82, fo. 65d; A.5/3, fo. 90d.
19. Ibid., A.1/47, fo. 32; A.5/3, fos 146, 149d–151; A.6/15, fos 54, 65d, 109d, 130d; A.6/16, fo. 91d.
20. Ibid., A.30/4, A.30/10.
21. Burley, *Servants*, 78–9.
22. *OSA*, vol. XVI, Sandwick and Stromness, 444–5; vol. XIX, Orphir, 406.
23. HBCA, B.59/b/14, fo. 1d; A.6/15 fo. 136; B.135/a/82, fo. 41d; A.6/16, fo. 40.
24. Ibid., E.41/3, fos 83–85.
25. Ibid., A.6/16, fos 50, 144d; A.6/17, fo. 51d; A.5/4, fo. 115; A.5/3, fo. 121d; E.41/3, fo. 88; A.10/1, fo. 51.
26. Ibid., A.1/48, fos 120–125; A.5/4, fos 135–137d, 143d–144; A.6/15, fo. 141; A.32/13; C.1/416, fo. 8; C.4/1, fo. 17.
27. Ibid., A.6/17, fos 66, 98; A.5/4, fos 156–156d; A.30/11.
28. Ibid., A.5/5, fo. 48d; A.6/18, fos 175–176; Bumsted, 'The Affair at Stornoway, 1811', 53; Burley, *Servants*, 4–5. Burley also provides an in-depth analysis of the 'New System' in *Servants*, 36–48.
29. HBCA, B.89/a/2, fos 1–36d; F.3/2, fos 108,113.
30. Ibid., A.10/1, fos 87–94; A.5/5, fo. 31; A.5/4, fo. 134; A.5/3, fo. 140d; A.36/1a fo. 20d; A.32/5; A.6/17, fo. 67.
31. Ibid., A.10/1, fos 87–94; B.198/b/4, fos 9–9d.
32. Ibid., A.6/18, fo. 175.
33. Ibid., A.6/18, fos 175–176; A.11/118, fo. 29d.
34. Ibid., A.6/18, fo. 27; A.5/5, fos 32–32d, 40d, 52d–53, 115, 129; A.32/40, fos 113–114; A.32/41, fo. 1; A.32/42, fo. 103; A.32/45, fo. 247; A.32/56, fo. 270; A.32/58, fos 57, 278; A.67/9, fo. 1; A.5/5, fo. 40d; A.16/15; A.6/19, fo. 99d. A.30/16; A.32/19, 23, 29, 41, 42, 47.
35. Ibid., A.30/15, fo. 33d–34; A.30/16, fo. 12.
36. Ibid., A.5/6, fo. 116d; J. P. Pritchett and F. J. Wilson, 'A Winter at Hudson Bay, 1811–12', *Canadian Historical Review*, 24: 1(1943), 5–11.
37. HBCA: A.1/51, fo. 20d.
38. Ibid., A.30/11; A.30/15; A.30/16.
39. Ibid., A.5/6, fos 87d, 109d, 112d.
40. Ibid., A.5/6, fos 149, 154d.
41. Ibid., A.5/6, fos 87d–162.
42. Olaf D. Cuthbert (ed.), *Low's History of Orkney* (Orkney, 2001), 37–86; *OSA*, vol. XX, St Andrews and Deerness, 259, 260, 268, 269; vol. XIV, Firth and Stenness, 130–2; vol. VII, Kirkwall and St Ola, 552, 540, 564, 569; vol. XIX, Orphir, 407, 419; vol. XV, South Ronaldsay and Burray, 301–2; vol. XVI, Sandwick and Stromness, 421–2, 466; vol. XVII, Walls and Flotta, 316–17; vol. XX, Evie and Rendall, 252–3.
43. Devine, *Scotland's Empire, 1600–1815*, 199.
44. HBCA, A.5/3, fo. 57d; A.1/48, fo. 120d.
45. Ibid., A.5/4, fos 113–113d, 129d–130, 137.
46. Ibid., A.5/4, fos 137–137d; A.6/15, fo. 114.
47. Ibid., A.5/3, fo. 27.
48. Brown, *Strangers In Blood*, 29.
49. HBCA, A.5/4, fo. 113.
50. Ibid., A.5/4, fos 113, 129d; A.30/16, fo. 23.
51. Burley, *Servants*, 167; HBCA, B.121/a/4, fo. 24.
52. Burley, *Servants*, 36–40; HBCA, A.16/13, fo. 97; A.30/15, fos 18d–19.

53. Brown, *Strangers In Blood*, 29; Sylvia Van Kirk, 'Fur Trade Social History: Some Recent Trends', in Carol M. Judd and Arthur J. Ray (eds), *Old Trails and New Directions: Papers of the Third North American Fur Trade Conference* (Toronto, 1980), 164.
54. HBCA, A.30/1, fo. 80d; A.30/10, fos 25d–26; A.30/11, fos 25d–26; A.32/2, fos 154, 166; A.32/4, fo. 146; A.32/6, fo. 46; B.121/a/4, fos 2,12, 20; HBC Biography, James Tait.
55. Ibid., A.5/4, fo. 35d; HBC Biography, Alexander Kennedy.
56. Ibid., A.30/10, fos 32d–33; A.30/11, fos 34, 36d–37; A.30/16; HBC Biography, James Kirkness, William Sinclair.
57. Ibid., A.6/18, fos 149–220, 244; A.30/16, fos 1–65; Burley, *Servants of the Honourable Company*, 37.
58. Ibid., HBC Biography, John Robertson; A.32/13, fo. 93.
59. Ibid., A.11/118, fo. 24; Brown, *Strangers In Blood*, 30.
60. HBCA, A.30/16, fos 1–65.
61. Ibid., A.30/15, fos 11d–12; A.30/16, fo. 61; A.30/17, fo. 1–2d.
62. Ibid., A.30/10, fos 3d, 8d, 21; A.6/17, fo. 68d.
63. Ibid., A.6/16, fo. 70d; A.5/3, fo. 72d; A.11/117, fo. 120; A.6/17, fo. 16–16d; A.30/10, fo. 5.
64. Glover, *Thompson's Narrative*, 17.
65. Glyndwr Williams (ed.), *Andrew Graham's Observations on Hudson's Bay, 1767–1791* (London, 1969), 299; HBCA, B.239/a/120, fo. 6d; D.1/11, fos 24d–25.
66. HBCA, A.30/16, fos 54d–55.
67. Ibid., B.239/a/92, fos 20d–21.
68. Ibid., B.3/a/120, fos 17–22; A.32/3, fo. 234; A.32/14, fo. 50, A.32/19, fo. 53d.
69. Ibid., B.59/a/94, fos 21d–22; Williams (ed.), *Andrew Graham's Observations*, 259, 299.
70. HBCA, B.59/b/28, fo. 5d B.3/z/2, fo. 303; B.42/z/1, fo. 4; B.176/a/1, fo. 2d; B.169/a/1, fo. 3d; B.177/a/6, fo. 5.
71. Ibid., B.3/z/2, fo. 303; B.42/z/1, fo. 4; B.59/b/30, fo. 8; B.176/a/1, fo. 2d; B.169/a/1, fo. 3d; B.177/a/6, fo. 5.
72. Ibid., B.23/a/10, fo. 3.
73. Ibid., B.177/a/1, fos 7d–10d.
74. Ibid., B.40/a/1, fo. 5.
75. Ibid., B.59/b/30, fos 8–9; B.3/z/2, fo. 303.
76. Ibid., B.40/a/1, fos 6d–15.
77. Ibid., B.141/a/1, fos 4–4d; B.164/a/1, fos 4–5d; B.3/a/115, fo. 12d; Burley, *Servants*, 164.
78. Ibid., B.3/a/120, fos 5d–13;
79. Ibid., fo. 35d; Burley, *Servants*, 215–17.
80. HBCA:, B.59/b/19, fo. 18.
81. *OSA*, vol. 20, St Andrews and Deerness, 265.
82. HBCA, A.6/14, fo. 30.
83. Ibid., A.5/4, fos 32d–34; A.16/15, fos 16d–17; A.30/16, fos 42–46; A.32/2, fo. 9; A.32/7, fo. 36; A.32/18, fo. 77; B.3/a/24, fos 24–25; B.59/b/13, fo. 7d; B.59/b/28, fo. 23; B.59/a/82, fos 9d, 20; B.121/a/7, fo. 5d; B.141/a/3, fo. 4; B.198/b/3, fos 1d, 9d; D.1/11, fo. 8.
84. Ibid., B.198/b/3, fo. 9d; B.59/b/13, fo. 7d.
85. Ibid., B.59/b/16, fo. 18d; B.135/a/80, fos 3–4; A.32/4, fo. 177.

86. William B. Ewart, 'Causes of Mortality in a Subarctic settlement (York Factory, Man), 1714–1946', *Canadian Medical Association Journal*, 129:6 (1983), 572; Burley, *Servants of the Honourable Company*, 131.
87. HBCA, B.3/a/120, fos 15d, 16, 21, 24d.
88. Ibid., A.11/117, fos 21d–22.
89. Ibid., fo. 61d. B.59/a/86, fos 31–31d.
90. Ibid., A.5/2, fos 137–138, 151–157, 176d; A.5/3, fos 54d–55d, 178d–179; A.5/5, fo. 103d; A.6/14, fo. 125; A.11/45, fo. 171.
91. Ibid., A.6/13, fo. 126d; A.5/6, fo. 86.
92. Ibid., A.6/13, fos 122d–134.
93. Ibid., A.5/5, fos 26–27.
94. Ibid., A.5/2, fo. 159.
95. Ibid., A.1/48, fos 60, 121; A.5/3, fo. 172d; A.5/5, fos 36d, 65; A.6/17, fo. 28d; A.16/7, fo. 19.
96. Brown, *Strangers In Blood*, 52–62; Sylvia Van Kirk, *'Many Tender Ties'. Women in Fur-Trade Society, 1670–1870* (Winnipeg, 1980), 4, 25–9, 38, 53–73; HBCA, B.177/a/5, fos 7d–9.
97. Brown, 51, 67; Van Kirk, *'Many Tender Ties'*, 4, 9, 27; William Newton, *Twenty Years on the Saskatchewan* (London, 1897), 39–40.
98. Brown, *Strangers In Blood*, 67.
99. HBCA:, A.6/19, fo. 48.
100. Van Kirk, *'Many Tender Ties'*, 35–6.
101. HBCA, A.5/6, fo. 76; A.5/5, fo. 2; B.3/a/118, fo. 3.
102. Ibid., A.16/6, fo. 150.
103. Ibid., A.16/15, fo. 38.
104. Ibid., A.6/17, fo. 66; A.5/4, fos 113d–130.
105. Ibid., A.16/15, fos 15, 36, 42.
106. *OSA*, vol. XIX, Orphir, 407; vol. XIV, Firth and Stenness, 133.
107. NAS, RS46/14/213 (1048); HBCA, A.30/11, fo 34; HBC Biography, William Sinclair.
108. NAS, CC8/8/135, fos 240–241; HBCA, HBC Biography, Magnus Twatt.

HIGHLAND EMIGRATION IN THE AGE OF MALTHUS: SCOURIE, 1841–55

ERIC RICHARDS

> Among the resident gentry, emigration to the colonies seems to be the sole remedy for the impending evil.
>
> Sir Edward Coffin, 1847[1]

I

At the time of the Potato Famine in the West Highlands of Scotland in the late 1840s, the doctrines of Robert Malthus loomed large among the men who controlled the fate of the region. Landlords, their factors and the relief administrators were acutely conscious of the danger that population would overreach the means of subsistence. Malthus had been reluctant to advocate emigration because, he declared, a vacuum was created which the natural forces of reproduction soon refilled. As emigrants departed their lots would be taken over by young couples who would soon increase the birth rate. He drew directly on recent population history to demonstrate his thesis, notably the experience of Jura and Skye where numbers grew phenomenally despite rapid emigration. But Malthus also said that the effect could be delayed by the prevention of reoccupation and the destruction of cottages.[2]

Emigration, as a response to famine, and as a cure-all for the long-term problems of poverty in the Highlands, was always contested by clergy, landowners, the estate tenantries, and political economists. Emigration was expensive, and also deeply divisive and unpredictable among the people themselves. The operation of the emigration solution was, in practice, an interplay of pressures, persuasion and demographic assumptions on both sides of the equation. The interior history of the emigration question was especially well-exposed in the fraught years of the famine.[3]

In the mid-nineteenth century the Highlands faced the consequences of the combined impact of two fundamental forces. First was unprecedented population growth which had accumulated since about 1780; second, there was the reduction of employment opportunities in the region.[4] These two forces had a scissors-like effect on the region and its people. It meant that there were too many people for the operation of the new economy dominated by sheep farming; a large proportion of the population was redundant. Many were living in rural squalor which had become a national disgrace. The effect was magnified because living standards in the rest of Scotland and Britain now rose each decade and the gap with the Highlands widened inexorably. Dependence on small crofts, a few animals, oats and potatoes made Highlanders highly vulnerable to harvest shortfall and poor prices for their livestock. The ways in which the region adjusted to this iron dilemma during the crisis of the potato famine is the focus of this paper.

What were the mechanisms? One was clearance and population displacement induced by the landlords. Another was demographic adjustment by way of reduced reproduction through later marriage and lower birthrates. Another was temporary migration to the south, which brought in money and reduced local dependence. A further and broader response was acceptance and fatalism which seemed to become entrenched in crofter communities, stoically living with adversity, praying for better times.

Finally, there was the solution urged upon the population by the rationalists of the day – namely the free flow of people out of the region and the natural readjustment of the population to the needs of the local labour market and current land use. The Highlands was a severe example of the problem of adjustment common to most rural districts in the British Isles: the general remedy advocated was the evacuation of labour. Emigration from the Highlands accelerated in the Famine years.[5]

The Scourie district in the far north-west corner of Sutherland (comprising the parishes of Assynt, Eddrachillis and part of Durness) was exceptionally well documented in terms of emigration and the tensions to which it gave rise. Typically the story derives from the records of the landowner, the second duke of Sutherland, and the voice of the prospective migrants is mostly unheard.[6] Scourie was a microcosm of the intersection of political, demographic and managerial forces which surrounded the decisions to accept or reject emigration. At the centre of the story was the collective psychology of people who were urged to evacuate their community, a dimension of the account often inaccessible in the study of emigration.

The context was one of restricted employment opportunities, narrowed further by the imposition of commercial sheep farming and deer forests.[7] The Scourie agency contained some of the most densely populated and poverty-ridden districts on the estate. The local management was devolved to agents who exerted immense authority (though ultimately answerable to the duke's commissioner, James Loch). The local factor, Evander McIver, was a Gaelic-speaking Lewisman, trained in farming in the lowlands, who had been appointed in 1845 and came to be regarded as the epitome of factorial dominance.[8] Always forthright and articulate, McIver believed that emigration was the prime solution to the problems of congestion and estate management.[9] His reports, sometimes verging on the splenetic, exposed the mechanisms at work in these west Highland communities. He worked to increase emigration, partly by persuading the duke to subsidise the costs of departure, and partly by exhorting the people to depart. He was at the very centre of this quasi-Malthusian process; in his hands the pressures of persuasion and coercion were carefully balanced. But they were also frustrated by the resistance of the people to the manipulation of the estate factor.

II

The Potato Famine spread into the West Highlands at the end of 1846 and there was no escape for Scourie. During the previous crisis, in 1837–8, the duke of Sutherland, following long tradition, had provided relief supplies and assisted emigration, especially to New South Wales.[10] In 1841 the local factor at Scourie, Alex Stewart, had advised the duke against any very active promotion of emigration. He said that there would be 'perfect embarrassment' if the duke fitted up a ship to take people to America: 'it would give the Public an idea that your Grace would be rather harshly turning off the Native Population in great numbers.' Sensitivity to public opprobrium was high: the Sutherland estate was already a target for much abuse in southern newspapers.[11] Stewart also warned of the psychological aspects of policies designed to assist or persuade prospective migrants. He said that 'As soon as intending parties to emigration would learn that your Grace was to do so much for them – they would slacken their exertions – not only in defraying the expense of embarkation – but in their Corner of the new Country'. The implication was that the people were crafty and unco-operative at best. Even more crucial was their attitude to emigration and the landlord: 'such is the case with the Highlanders – that if they conceive a Landlord is very urgent to get quit of them – the more they cling to their present places – at least this is the result of my experience with other Highlanders and I believe it to be exactly the same in Sutherland.' James Loch, commissioner to the far-flung Sutherland estates, agreed with this interpretation of local attitudes when he ordered: 'ask no one to go – and allow none the full cost of entire passage but assist those who are desirous to go.' In this case the landlord was exceedingly keen to encourage emigration, which was regarded by the administration as beneficial to all parties, notably the landlord himself. More particularly, Loch enunciated a doctrine derived from Malthus himself:[12] if emigration was to have the desired effect of curbing population congestion, the vacated lands should not be allowed to regenerate population growth. As Loch instructed explicitly, 'You had better pull down the house [of a departing emigrant] and give the materials to the neighbors'. Otherwise the benefit would be lost.[13]

Before the first onset of the potato failure in 1845, Stewart had been succeeded by Evander McIver who made almost daily reports throughout the crisis.[14] The factors, as well as James Loch, were extremely concerned that the people of the west coast were becoming permanently dependent on the landlord; they saw the danger of an ever-recurring cycle of destitution which his policies should be designed to break. It was fully consistent with prevailing Malthusian sentiment. Consequently relief was to be determined by need: the able bodied would be required to work for their subsistence. This, together with the long-term benefit of the estate, was the guiding principle. But relief was to be combined with the encouragement of emigration, thought to be a more permanent solution to the long-term malaise of the district. McIver believed that the people were idle and that his district was 'lightly rented and it is quite disgraceful to its tenantry that arrears should exist'.[15] Moreover the people expected gratuitous supplies: they were told that 'all who can work must be employed and the weak and helpless on the Poor Roll must be supplied'.[16] McIver also reported that efforts to encourage recruitment into the regiments had been unsuccessful: 'The prejudice to the army and navy existing in the minds of the people of the whole North of Scotland is very surprising – considering the poverty and hardships they live in and are exposed to at home.' He advised the duke to avoid all connection with recruitment: 'any anxiety on the part of your Grace or your agents would only make them suspect it was a plot to get rid of them'.[17] It equally affected their attitude to emigration and was an unambiguous legacy of the clearances earlier in the century, reinforcing the prevailing mentality of mistrust and suspicion.[18]

In August 1846 McIver had been in Skye and Barra where he was shocked by the blackened state of the potato crops which he believed threatened actual starvation unless relief was provided.[19] Within a week the disease was all over Assynt. He warned the duke that 'It will require great caution for the people are already impressed with the idea that your Grace is to the assist them very liberally'.[20] The duke, phenomenally wealthy, had declined financial assistance from the various philanthropic Destitution Committees at work in the Highlands. He chose to shoulder the burden of relief from his own estate resources (though he later did take advantage of the terms of the Drainage Act). A combination of genuine concern and aristocratic hubris caused the duke to assume total responsibility for the people of the estate.[21] He was already committed to heavy expenditures to relieve the local crisis: he was able to draw upon his vast income in the south and was in a better position than most other landlords. He made a personal commitment to succour the people throughout the crisis: he was prepared to ensure food supplies, to provide employment on special projects and, more particularly, to subsidise emigration. The expenditure was greatly in excess of rent income and there was an adamant determination that no lives would be lost in the crisis.[22]

Echoing Malthus, Loch told the duke of Sutherland in October 1846 that 'The difficulty with whole country is overpopulation, which is encreased by the kindness with which they are treated.' It was vital for the future progress of the country that the duke's kindness in the crisis should not encourage them 'to look to you and not to themselves for their maintenance.' He also asserted that any subsidies of food prices at below market rates would undoubtedly 'paralise the exertions of the industrious and encourage the less active.' He felt it necessary, for the better future of the people themselves, to resist the duke's spontaneous generosity.[23] As Loch told Sir David Dundas, MP for Sutherland, 'his extreme benevolence would often induce him to interfere in trying to help them, to an extent that would virtually be to their own harm... they are indolent like all people – they would rather beg than work'.[24] The duke in the outcome rejected some of Loch's more rigorous doctrines, saying, for instance, that crofters in Assynt could not pay as much for food as people in Yorkshire or Manchester, simply because they did not have comparable employment.[25] McIver told the duke that he should not visit the district: 'The people would torment and annoy Your Grace with their distress – and in summer when your Grace revisits the Country I am sure they will be very presuming and troublesome'.[26]

In January 1847 McIver reported that there was plenty of meal available though the price was high. He reported that 'the importunities of the people are very harassing'.[27] Already he had instituted relief works, trenching and road building, which would provide those in need with the capacity to feed themselves through the crisis. McIver believed the situation in his district was serious but manageable, though there were problems working with the meal dealers whose trade was disrupted by the duke's interventions. He exclaimed, 'How thankful we should be when we compare our situation with that of the Irish Peasantry!'[28]

McIver drew up a manifesto of the thinking behind the relief system. The duke would 'find and provide food for the people'; he would also find employment for 'those who are willing an able to work' at a penny per hour,[29] so that 'payment can be procured from them'.[30] The employment schemes were designed for 'taking in more lands and draining and trenching' from which 'we can expect to make the country produce a sufficiency of food for the support of the people'. But this was to be 'coupled with a regular system of Emigration and increased industry in fishing on the part of those who remain.' The long-run solution to the problems of the district was a reduced population which would be established on a firmer base created by the relief measures; 'it would 'tend materially to improve the condition of the Small Tenants – it must be the result of years of systematic management and large outlays.' But most fundamentally it required a smaller population and emigration to which McIver set his mind, realising that the outcome would not be easily achieved.[31] McIver evidently conceived this as a grand plan to make his district pay.[32]

With emigration in the background, relief measures were instituted and McIver reported, 'Luckily my district was never healthier than it is now – and thanks to your Grace's liberality there is no want.' The duke's generosity was partly facilitated by the terms of the Drainage Act which subsidised landlords' efforts, yielding permanent improvements to estates.[33] By mid-March 1847 McIver was employing 600 to 700 men in his district and had brought in 7,699 bolls of food from various sources including Banff, Liverpool, Aberdeen and Glasgow.[34] This was full-scale and prompt famine relief reinforced by the payment of one pound to each man searching for work in the south.[35] A visiting ship's crew, recently in Ireland, was 'much struck with the robust and healthy appearance of the people here, and are amazed not to have seen a Beggar since they arrived. My whole district never was healthier, and no wonder when one thinks of the good food they are living on'.[36]

Relief measures were expensive (though kept at a minimum by a work requirement for the able bodied) but mostly temporary in their benefits. More permanent, though also expensive, was emigration, which offered a diminution of the dependent population once and for all.[37] The Malthusian 'vacuum' effect was counteracted by the parallel policy which amalgamated vacated lots and prohibited subdivision, both designed to deter early marriages.[38] But McIver was careful: 'I have studiously avoided the subject of Emigration with the people, convinced any overture on the subject from me or any person in your Grace's service would have an injurious effect'.[39]

Emigration was in the air. 'There is talk as to Emigration in Assynt', said McIver, 'and it will be good policy to encourage them liberally.'[40] Canada was favoured over other possibilities, including the Australian option. James Loch had seen a pamphlet encouraging emigration with assistance on good terms to South Australia. But McIver told the duke that 'a deep rooted prejudice exists in the minds of the people to any part of Australia. Nothing I say can make any impression. Such is the prejudice in the mind of an ignorant man.'[41] McIver told the duke that 'Emigration is the most politic relief and our utmost energies must be applied to stimulate the people to go. America is the country they will go to from this District.' Timing was also critical: once the small tenants had begun 'to till their crofts, departed to the fishing or to the south, then the season for emigration had passed.' This had happened by March 1847 but McIver had better hopes for the next season when 'a large number will take advantage of your Grace's liberality' – and he intended to 'feel the pulse of the people' before engaging any ship for emigration.[42]

The suggestibility of the Scourie people to emigration became a critical factor during the ensuing years in which McIver attempted to promote the policy of emigration. There were eddying psychological currents in operation over which he had little control. But he knew that the people could not be coerced and he had to avoid giving any impression of pushing them into emigration. Emigration also involved complicated negotiations with shippers and governmental agencies which provided part of the subsidies for the passages, to which the duke now made large contributions.[43] McIver was anxious to accelerate emigration and was aware of the seasonal elements in the decisions to migrate: 'I so hope most anxiously that some definite resolution as to Emigration were come to, the people will be in the course of a week or ten days beginning to cultivate their lots, and once they engage in this they abandon all idea of emigrating this year.' The cost of passage was variable and now the expense of provisions had to be added: McIver remarked, 'If I could now intimate that both would be paid I think a number would go this year,' which suggests that poverty was the primary restraint on emigration. One of the local Free Church ministers, the Reverend Tulloch, also became involved and declared that the people were expecting the Government to provide aid directly for emigration to America; they were disconcerted by the intervention of the duke.

By April 1847 McIver was able to say, 'I have succeeded beyond my expectation as in the Emigration Scheme. The list now numbers including young and old 378 souls – the proportion of which from Assynt is small, and as I anticipated none from Knockan and Elphin. I have intimated that I cannot exceed 400 in number – and as I was sure that they had no provisions of their own in place of giving £2 to each, I have only promised as much meal as the voyage may require – this may cost about 24/- to each individual – and the balance of 16/- will carry them up to Canada – but I have not yet told them they are to get this – in some instances I have promised a pair of shoes and two cotton shirts to the children. Some blankets for the poorest would be a great boon. I have written to Liverpool, Newcastle and Aberdeen about a vessel – and if I find it necessary will go myself in search of one. I hear that freights are high owing to the demand for vessels for carrying grain provisions'.[44]

McIver had expected the Reverend Tulloch to encourage the emigration but he suddenly turned into an opponent of the emigration. 'He told one of the men who is to emigrate he had known people who went from Caithness glad to return again. The Free Church Ministers who depend on the people for their sustenance are not likely to give much encouragement to emigrate.' Such were the rising tensions surrounding the organisation of emigration, but it is clear that many of the people were extremely poor and that the landlord was prepared to subsidise their evacuation very readily.

By March weather conditions had improved and McIver reported that a thaw had begun; a consignment of Norwegian potatoes had also arrived. Meanwhile the 'Emigration List' had increased to 400. Emigrant-carrying vessels were scarce and freight costs rose steeply. A vessel for Pictou in Nova Scotia had arrived at Loch Laxford and would soon be dispatched. McIver had to report that 'a few of those who agreed to go by her have withdrawn back – which is most provoking,' though 'a large proportion will however go and they are preparing for the change.' It was part of the psychology of emigration – poor people desperately worrying and wavering about the decision to emigrate and thereby upsetting McIver's elaborate plans. Another vessel was being readied for Montreal and McIver told the duke that he did not want him in the district till she was away 'as my whole time must be devoted to the Emigrants'.[45]

We possess no direct evidence that the famine crisis loosened the people's ties with the land and thereby promoted emigration.[46] But it is clear that during these years the landlord not only became more urgent to dispose of and disperse the people, but was also more generous and pressing with assistance for their departure. The people may have become more responsive to the idea; more significantly, the poorest of them were now provided with the means of doing so and this was probably most decisive in the process.

Amid the flurry of emigration, estate management continued in its usual business. McIver arranged a small but aggravated removal at this time and precipitated the predictable reaction among the people concerned, that is, the women mounted an alarming degree of resistance to the sheriff officer. The duke expressed doubt about the wisdom of the removal but McIver was adamant about its necessity.[47] McIver, angered by the turn of events, declared that his authority with the people would be undermined if the duke intervened.[48] The duke was extremely dubious about eviction and was clearly at odds with his factor.

III

At the end of 1847 the murrain again attacked potato crops across the West Highlands; in Scourie the employment measures were reinforced and food supplies again secured at market prices (despite difficult negotiations with the dealers). There was a great demand for meal and credit in the district.[49] At the end of December the duke of Sutherland authorised McIver to arrange for another vessel to sail to Canada if enough intending emigrants came forth.[50] The mood of the people seemed to shift and now there was a marked, but unstable enthusiasm, for emigration. In February 1848 McIver reported to the duke that he did not 'think your Grace would enjoy being at Laxford (the port of embarkation) when a ship was about to sail with emigrants. I seldom had a more painful and disagreeable task – the parting with their friends and their native country when it came was really sad – nothing but the conviction that it was for the good of the people themselves carried me through it'.[51]

Despite such melancholy scenes there was a rising clamour for assisted emigration to Canada. McIver had received eight letters, interesting and satisfactory, from previous migrants from Assynt to Canada and he wanted them printed and circulated ('the tone of all has been favourable').[52] 'A great many are talking of it,' he reported. Already there were more applicants than he had anticipated: 'The emigration is now a sore subject to me. I did all in my power to foster it – and now that the people are really anxious to go the expense so far exceeds what I ever dreamt of or thought of, that I feel most uneasy and most vexed about it – and added to this I am kept in constant turmoil by the Emigrants who crowd round me wherever I go'; there would be no relief until 'these poor people sail.' Loch had estimated the cost to the duke at £6 per emigrant (McIver had thought £5 closer to the mark). He predicted that if the potato again failed in 1849 a great majority of the people of Assynt would want to emigrate 'if they could get away'. Managing emigration was evidently a complicated matter. In

April 1848 McIver was refusing some of the applicants: some had withdrawn but there were many more wanting to go. The remaining households on the island of Handa, impoverished by the famine, had resolved to depart (McIver himself took over the island).[53] Two ships at Laxford, sailing to Pictou and Quebec, were being readied and, by mid-June, 574 people had departed.[54]

McIver connected emigration with a policy of rationalising the population. He was particularly engaged in an attempt to remove twenty-four tenants from the remaining inland townships of Knockan and Elphin. 'It is likely that some of the old people must be left while they live', he explained. The others might be resettled within the estate though he 'hoped the surplus will emigrate from Knockan and Elphin – if not, there will be lots in other places in Assynt vacated by [other] Emigrants. None will emigrate to Australia – there is a very strong prejudice – all prefer America'. It was clear that the older members of the population were opposed to any sort of emigration; and the people of Elphin and Knockan were notoriously resistant to removal of any sort. McIver was angered and stymied.[55]

In early 1848 an independent scrutiny of the local relief system was instituted at the behest of the duke of Sutherland. Captain Robert Elliott RN was Inspector-General of Highland Destitution, Edinburgh, and in March 1848 he spent nine days in Scourie and Tongue specifically seeking out the 'most minute investigation into the condition of *many* of those considered most destitute'.[56] In the outcome his glowing report commended the duke's efforts, which amounted to 'the entire care of preventing loss of life, by starvation on his estates.' He was impressed by 'the gigantic and expensive efforts which the duke made for the relief of Destitution with such generosity and success.' Elliott roundly condemned the indolence and ingratitude of the small tenantry, their indulgence in improvident marriages, and their neglect of education; he described 'townships... swarming with breechless vagabonds hereditarily idle.' They received extraordinary 'parental' care from the duke which was often not appreciated. Indeed 'the people had never been better fed than with the duke of Sutherland's meal last year', and rents were low. The petitions of complaint by the people, he asserted, 'originated in avarice and deceit, and are not borne out by facts or necessity.'[57] He strongly supported the 'destitution' work test on moral and economic grounds. In the Scourie district, the duke had spent no less than £17,719, in addition to £10,441 on meal, £2,000 on emigration, as well £27,000 on normal expenses. Across his entire Sutherland estate, with a rent roll of £39,000, the duke had spent £78,000 which did not include expenditure on the current rebuilding programme at Dunrobin Castle.[58] McIver reflected that Elliott's *Report* would 'strengthen our hands in dealing firmly with the people.'

IV

Throughout the famine years the Sutherland estate administration simultaneously wrestled with relief measures, removals, food supply and emigration in a context in which the prospective migrants fluctuated in their interest and resolution. Their determination was not helped by contradictory reports received from recent migrants to Canada. One of the previous Handa migrants, Hector Falconer, who had sailed to Pictou on the *Ellen* in 1848 (described by McIver as 'a cautious man – and I am satisfied he states the truth'), sent back 'not very flattering' reports regarding Prince Edward Island. The voyage of five weeks had been successful, and all the passengers were healthy and in good spirits apart from the death of one old widow. But on arrival the local authorities had exacted double 'head money' from the immigrants, impounded their luggage and left them in distress. Falconer also described the raw reality of an immigrant's start in the new country: though he had access to land he had reaped no crop or income for a year: 'I did not earn a shilling since I came to this country' and 'people coming here destitute of means to support themselves [in] the first year . . . find it very difficult till they get a crop raised . . . so that I could not conceivably encourage any man to come here, . . . still to give proper justice to the country it is a better country for a poor man [but] . . . there has been a failure of the Crop these past three years, that left everything dull in this place.'[59] The irony was that these migrants were entering a colony affected by precisely the same famine from which they were fleeing – and from which previous Highland emigrants, who had arrived three decades before, were themselves dramatically re-emigrating to the Antipodes.[60]

The variability in the responses to emigration opportunities were exemplified by concurrent reports from the east coast of the Sutherland estate. The local factor George Gunn remarked, 'Our people are so wavering, that no experience of their habits will enable one to dive into their projects or to judge of what country they are likely to follow – last year . . . they had a decided prejudice against New Zealand – New South Wales or any such distant colony – no place for them like Canada – while now, the tide runs in full force in favour of Australia. I believe some hundreds of them are preparing and have entered their names to emigrate to that place, and it will be a good riddance and an easy way to get clear of them, and the utmost we shall have to pay is for their passage by sea to Leith, a mere trifle in comparison with the charge for taking them to Canada'. Gunn then described the dissimulation he employed in the business of emigration: 'I continue the policy I have already mentioned to your Grace, to seem indifferent whether they go or remain, I [therefore] know little of what the ultimate result of this move will be'.[61]

In Scourie the potato crop failed for a third time in October 1848 and the relief measures were repeated, now reinforced by loans from the Drainage Act and the import of more meal into the district. The local factors were irritated by the fact that fishing crews from as far away as Buckie were fishing off the Sutherland coasts and selling fish to the local land-bound natives. The factors declared that it was vital 'to make the people depend more on themselves', or, preferably, emigrate.[62]

Two years later further contradictory reports began to arrive back in the Scourie district concerning the fate of earlier emigrants to Canada. McIver had to tell the duke that the people who left in 1848 were not happy and that their letters home were neither cheering nor encouraging. On the other hand letters from those who reached better lands in Upper Canada were 'very encouraging'. Letters were being received with every steamer from those who had emigrated during the previous two years and they also carried highly variable reports.[63] McIver reiterated his belief that 'Emigration is the greatest boon a Proprietor can confer on such Tenants we have to deal with.' He pointed out the new Poor Law for the relief of the able-bodied was imminent and that it was 'true policy to get as many away as possible before it comes into operation.' He was also persuading a Shetland Fishing company to maintain their fishing operations along the local coastline so that there would be 'a strong argument for me in testing applications for relief.' His clear priority was to reduce the level of dependency among the population under his factorship.[64]

In the winter months of 1849–50 the continuing famine conditions in the Scourie district did not diminish: 'the cry for food and employment is becoming daily more urgent,' reported McIver, 'and I believe there is more real necessity for it now than since the Potato failure came on in this District.'[65] Meal supplies were continuing to reach his locality and many young men were traveling to Caithness to find good wages and cheap meal even though 'the severity of the weather keeps them very frequently from work.'

Prospective emigrants in Assynt were now actively petitioning for help to emigrate and, realising that they possessed a certain leverage in the matter, were prepared to bargain over the terms of their emigration. In mid April McIver was surprised to receive a large deputation from Assynt. They represented '300 souls who were most anxious to go'. When the duke offered to pay half of the costs of the passage and provisions for each person in a family he was told that very few would accept such terms.[66] Meanwhile the government was offering assistance to Irish emigrants and McIver hoped that the same terms would be extended to the West Highlanders. Calculated bargaining attended both sides of the equation: the estate knew that it would gain from the reduction of the population; the people understood they had value as emigrants and were prepared to use their bargaining power to extract the best assistance from the landlord. The basic problem was that 'the terms of the passage by Mr Sutherland, Wick, for the passage to America were so high that not one family from the District ... can muster sufficient means, even with the liberal aid offered to emigrate this year.' This demonstrated the fundamental difficulty, namely that the poorest of the community, those whom the factors most wished to lose, were least able to undertake emigration.[67] Sheer poverty stood in the way of prospective emigrants, even where the landlord offered considerable subsidies. This was the Malthusian trap: emigration, to which Malthus had given merely equivocal sanction, remained an expensive solution for all parties. Fine calculations were made on both sides of the negotiation and by May 1849 it became clear that the terms for the Atlantic passage offered by the shipping agent in Wick were too high and there was little emigration in that year.[68]

The Free Church ministers were also influential. Some of them, according to McIver, would gladly accompany the people to America simply because their own funding was diminishing with the outflow of emigrants. But so long as the Free Church headquarters in Edinburgh was prepared to pay the income of the country ministers 'few will be found willing to make the sacrifice and go to America for the sake of the people – till compelled to do so by a large falling off in the amount of their salaries.' This was the typically cynical view of the Free Ministers by the Scourie factor.[69]

McIver made no bones about the context of emigration. In April 1850, he told the duke that 'There is no doubt much poverty now among our lotters. They are each becoming poorer and the prospects this season are most discouraging. The Herring fishing on the Caithness Coast, which used to be the principal stay of a large majority especially in Assynt, is not likely to be resorted to this year by many.' Moreover cattle prices were low, and this was 'a most ruinous consideration'. These people included descendants of the interior people who had been resettled on the coasts during the clearances of the early part of the century, at a time of rapid population growth. Whatever the original cause of their current poverty,[70] these communities were now compacted along the coast in settlements which, in the difficult mid-century years, were evidently unable to support them with any security.

McIver said that without further relief employment provided by the Sutherland Estate 'there would be a loud cry of want'. The work allowed the people to support their families but they had too little income from which to pay their rents: 'The low price of meal is the greatest mercy [which] enables many to earn what feeds in comfort their whole families. The prospects for the future are however very gloomy indeed'. According to McIver the people each year were becoming poorer and poorer; extracting any rent from them was becoming increasingly difficult.[71] Conditions in the district were not uniform – Durness seemed to be improving, but Assynt not at all: 'the population is so dense that I don't look for improvement in their condition... I found a strong desire for emigration had arisen in consequence of some encouraging accounts from those who had gone two years ago to Upper Canada.' He expected about four families from Elphin, an inland township with good grazings, to leave.[72]

James Loch was of a mind with McIver. Writing from Dublin during a tour of Ireland, he told the duke that he was 'quite sure you cannot do better than help the West Country people to emigrate – taking care that the land they leave is properly disposed of. It is wonderful the extent to which Emigration is taking place from Ireland.' From Kilrush to Shannon he had witnessed 'The leave taking [which] were of the most touching nature. They get not only the most pressing letters from their relatives but large remittances to take them out. They all go to the States... this drain on the population will tell materially in the situation of this country.' Loch was critical of the way in which so much of the Irish population had become dependent on the potato and in which the landlords seemed to connive, unlike Sutherland, he asserted.[73]

Conditions in north-west Sutherland began gradually to improve in 1850 though the resort to emigration continued to oscillate and left the local agents perplexed. In May McIver reported that employment opportunities were available, food prices were lower and 'The country never was healthier'.[74] While destitution receded the bedrock poverty of the people on the coast continued. According to McIver they were each year becoming poorer and the prospects were extremely discouraging. Getting any rent from them was very difficult. He said that if the duke ceased to assist them 'they will all became paupers'.[75] In the following year the crops again improved and he could say that they were 'not so deep in Meal accounts as for some years'.[76] The factors were bent on the longer-run solution which still gave priority to the promotion of emigration and the division of Assynt townships into crofts. McIver reported 'very gratifying accounts for the Emigrants. They sailed in good spirits'. And in September 1850 the duke provided further funds to help some of the poorest to reach Upper Canada.

Attitudes to emigration remained extremely volatile. For instance, the people of Kinlochbervie were adamant about the subject. The duke was told that 'Even if your Grace were disposed to aid them to emigrate they have no desire to go – no persuasion or remonstrance will induce them to alter their mode of cropping or get into some better mode of culture.' To their own frustration the factors were able to promote neither improvement nor emigration.

But there were further shifts in the winds of migration. News of gold discoveries in Australia quickly reached the Highlands and new assistance schemes gave added enticement. The Australian colonies offered extremely generous assistance and the Sutherland estate, and other highland landlords, were keen to co-operate.[77] The operations of the Highland and Island Emigration Society co-ordinated substantial outflows between 1847 and 1855. The people were evidently aware that the Sutherland estate wanted them to emigrate and continued to bargain for assistance. In March 1852 Loch wrote to the agent for the Australian colonies that 'there is now exhibited a greater desire for emigration in the [extreme?] parts of Sutherland, than prevailed last year... the time is therefore perhaps arrived when you may prevail upon them to go, if you could pay them another visit – and you may perhaps find it necessary to promise them a little more assistance than you did at first.'[78] Emigration to America remained an option and prospective migrants hoped to get their entire expenses paid by the duke and 'they waited for this, and delayed their emigration as a consequence.' Loch pointed out that 'the less they will go for, the greater will be the number that you can send out'.[79]

Emigration was therefore a matter of careful bargaining and delicate diplomacy among the several parties to the process. If the duke seemed to press emigration it would deter the prospective emigrants. When James Loch urged an agent of the colonies to recruit migrants it was essential that he kept his distance from the estate administration—there was a danger of 'being misunderstood' both locally and in the press.[80] This suggests a degree of self-determination among the people departing: they did not want to appear to be coerced or bribed into emigration. The duke made covert subventions to the costs of emigration, anxious not to be seen to influence the flow. Nor could emigration be associated with clearance.[81] In essence it became necessary to mask or disguise the participation of the landlord in the process of emigration. This was at the heart of the psychology of migration in the Scourie District: the people resisted the pressure to go; if they decided to go they extracted the best terms. They rejected the idea that their interests were identical with those of the landlord.

Emigration agents perambulating the region were an object of cynicism among the people: the common suspicion was that they were in league with the landlords who were keen to take advantage of the emigration schemes, reducing their own financial commitment. When John Sutherland, employed by the government emigration commissioners in Wick, visited the Scourie District he was assured that he was no longer in 'danger to his being considered the dukes agent'.[82] It was imperative that he avoid the company of the estate factors for fear of 'the appearance of being the duke's agent'.[83] The duke was prepared to offer the prospective emigrants £1 per head to help them to get to the ports of embarkation, but it could only be done indirectly through an agent and without public acknowledgement. It was a mark of the delicate and temperamental status of attitudes on the estate at the moment when very poor people made the most important decision of their lives.

George Gunn, who was McIver's counterpart in the Sutherland estate management in Dunrobin, certainly regarded emigration to the colonies as a way of relieving the dead weight of poverty. In April 1852 Gunn described the 'wretchedly poor people' of Lothbeg, subtenants who included the large young family of Widow Bannerman who lived in 'thatched premises'. Emigration, he asserted, would 'get rid of the whole beggarly set for a far less outlay than will be required to help in building them houses as was promised, besides that will relieve the Estate from what will be a heavy incubus on it for a generation to come.' The whole population was 'troublesome [and] quarreling' and there was no end to the problem. An incoming large tenant had been promised clear access; emigration was a solution to the 'question ... how are they to be disposed of.' It was a managerial mentality mutually reinforced among the factors of the estate.[84]

In March 1853 Robert Horsburgh, McIver's counterpart in the Tongue management, reported continuing interest in emigration to Australia. But it was 'unfortunately as yet confined almost entirely to single young men, and these are exactly the parties to whom free passages appear to be refused.' The colonies, as well as the estate, wanted families to migrate, specifically for their cohesive qualities which made them less likely to rush off to the goldfields. The duke had made £100 available to lubricate the process; and Horsburgh pointed out that migration to the south was desirable but not so effective as emigration since the people might easily return home and again sink into dependence.[85] When the Australian colonies suddenly reduced their agencies in the north, the duke continued to offer aid to emigrants, but the impetus was lost. As Loch remarked to one of his sons, 'It is a pity that this emigration scheme is stopt. We could have sent out some fine highland colonists, good shepherds, good spadesmen, excellent wall builders'.[86]

The Highland and Island Emigration Society had effectively made emigration to Australia virtually free and organised 5,000 passages from across the region. Most of the project worked well enough but several of the ships ran into misfortunes, most notably the *Hercules* which was wracked by storms and disease. When news of the horrors experienced by the Skye people aboard the *Hercules* reached Scotland there was a rapid decline in candidates for migration. Robert Horsburgh from Tongue reported:

> The truth is, that I very much fear few or none of the folk in my district will now avail themselves of free passages to Australia!! The disasters of the Skye people have created much alarm, while several of them who formerly applied have gone to work in the south. Besides single young men not in families in which women predominate, and couples with many young children, are entirely cut out by the Regulations.[87]

Highland emigration to Australia was not sustained beyond the crisis.

Estate administration returned to its previous priorities. McIver was determined to control and rationalise his district and this involved recurrent small-scale removals, now the most contentious aspect of estate administration. In March 1853 he again received a sharp rebuke from the duke for arranging a process of removal to be brought against a tenant without his specific approval: it was clearly a matter of public reputation; the duke's imperative was that in such cases the Small Debts Court be employed without recourse to a summons of removal. The duke at all times tried to dissociate himself from the legacy of the clearances. Even ostensibly straightforward cases of removal all too often attracted bad publicity. But the exhortation to emigrate and the expenditures on local improvements continued unabated. Yet the outcome was disappointing to James Loch, now in the last years of his life. He told McIver, somewhat forlornly, that 'your district has been relieved to some extent by the Emigration that took place some time back – but I cannot admit that its effects are more than of a temporary nature and a perpetuation of such expenditures cannot be undertaken'.[88] This was a truly Malthusian commentary on the intervening efforts.

In the outcome, there was considerable emigration out of Assynt in these years though typically there are no precise numbers. The census figures show that the population of Assynt indeed fell, though only slightly, from 1841 to 1851. Assynt's population in 1861 was almost exactly as it had been in 1841. Emigration apparently siphoned off much of the natural increase during these decades; without emigration the increase would have been much greater (as it had been between 1811 and 1841).[89] Moreover the sex imbalance in the Assynt population in 1861 demonstrated the impact of differential migration (either seasonal or permanent) among young males.[90] But the results were much smaller than hoped for by McIver and the estate in general. The effect of emigration across rural Britain tended to be gradual and cumulative and variable. In the case of Assynt the great absolute decline of population was delayed until after 1901. Until then the west coast experience seemed to confirm Malthus' pessimism about the permanent benefits of emigration; but then the nexus with the pre-industrial past, and with Malthus, was finally broken.

V

Over several generations the people of the West Highlands had found little benefit from the revolution in economic productivity in the British Isles at the time of industrialisation. The great new sheep economy reduced employment and access to the land and meanwhile the population multiplied with little measurable restraint. The narrow communities were left marginalised and without local solutions to their plight.[91] There was little attempt at co-operation between the people and the landlords as they confronted the problem of poverty, famine and destitution. The alleviation of highland poverty eventually entailed the reduction of the population to the point which allowed highland incomes to converge towards higher national averages. This entailed an equalisation of differentials of income and wealth (both present and prospective), with Highlanders moving to higher income regions in a generally rational fashion. The process was a long delayed and resisted adjustment. Coerced evacuation occurred and pressure was exerted in many less obvious ways. It is well known that during the famine decade, in many but not all districts, there was a significant acceleration of emigration and a faster detachment of the people from the land. It appeared to be a mechanical Malthusian evacuation, people fleeing in the face of adversity, deciding that there was no decent future in the Highlands.

The Scourie case suggests that the adjustment operated in unpredictable and even capricious ways. There were radically different levels of emigration even between adjacent districts and this extreme variability is not easily sheeted home to any precise structural differences between parishes, such as rental pressure, population congestion, hunger, subdivision and clearances.[92] The internal evidence from the factors' own offices shows that the pressures were exerted indirectly (indeed eviction was effectively prohibited by the landlord); and the blandishments of the landlord were often resisted. Beyond the goad of destitution, the critical factors included the flow of news from previous emigrants and, more particularly, the provision of unprecedentedly favourable assistance towards the costs of emigration. Poverty was always the greatest impediment to emigration. Emigrant letters enhanced the promise of emigration; generous assistance reduced the cost of emigration for prospective emigrants. This helped to budge rural inertia while also releasing the grip of poverty which impeded departure. In the case of Scourie there was a robust interplay of the forces of persuasion and retention, of push and pull, operating on the people of this district. Most of all it was about the social psychologies of the managers and the people, the prospective candidates for emigration.

The mid-century investigations into the West Highlands were preludes to the more intensive enquiry into crofting conditions in the 1880s by Lord Napier's Commission. They were generally highly critical of the capacity of crofting to sustain adequate living standards among the existing population of the Highlands. They recommended much increased emigration as a solution.[93] This prescription was warmly rejected by the alternative school of thought which maintained that, with better access to landed resources, more education and encouragement, the crofters could support themselves in decent comfort.[94] This division of opinion about emigration was not exclusive to the Highlands, of course, and was paralleled by the concurrent debate in Ireland.

Testifying before the Napier Commission, thirty years after the famine, Evander McIver continued to believe that emigration was the best solution, and that preferably half of the entire population should leave his district. But McIver declared that he had not been able to hasten the process nor even to prevent subdivision and sub-letting. As for the people, their spokesmen continued to believe that emigration was unnecessary simply because they had been dispossessed of the land.[95] The general view was that they were being pressed into emigration essentially because they had lost access to the land during the clearances – and that the return of their land would obviate any need to emigrate. The actual causes and trajectories of Highland emigration were less straightforward. As this paper suggests, there was a fine line between the exercise of free choice and the pressure of local conditions in the decision to emigrate.[96]

Notes

1. Quoted in Malcolm Gray, *The Highland Economy, 1750–1850* (Edinburgh, 1957), 189.
2. This question is considered in Eric Richards, 'Malthus and the Uses of British Emigration', in Andrew S. Thompson and Kent Fedorowich (eds), *Empire, Identity and Migration in the British World* (forthcoming, Manchester, 2011). Note that the vacuum effect was raised explicitly in the Parliamentary Papers [P.P.], 1841, VI, *First Report from the Select Committee on Emigration, Scotland, 1841*, q. 398. Evander McIver gave evidence with a clear statement of his attitude to emigration, q. 1276–1399.
3. E. A. Wrigley has argued that Malthusian ideas applied mostly to pre-industrial populations and this gives extra significance to the West Highland case. See E. A. Wrigley, 'Elegance and Experience: Malthus at the Bar of History,' in David Coleman and Roger Schofield (eds), *The State of Population Theory: Forward from Malthus* (Oxford, 1986), 46ff.

    'Interior' is used in the sense of the psychology of the emigration decision – an allusion to Voltaire who wanted to know 'how men lived in the interior of their families'; quoted by Eric Richards, 'Hearing Voices', in A. James Hammerton and Eric Richards (eds), *Speaking to Immigrants* (Canberra, 2002), 15.

4. The *Statistical Account of Scotland, 1791–1799* testified to the insecurity of the crops in the late eighteenth century in the parishes of Assynt, Eddrachillis and Durness; it especially noted the much increased dependence on potatoes. The existence of a substantial middling element in the social structure was also apparent; particular emphasis was accorded to the manner in which families looked after their own poor, and the old and infirm. Sir John Sinclair (ed.), *Statistical Account of Scotland, 1791–1799* (reprinted Wakefield, 1979), vol. XVIII, 302–3, 313–14, 376–7, 385, 393, 404–6.
5. See T. M. Devine, *The Great Highland Famine* (Edinburgh, 1988), Preface and 68–9.
6. The main exceptions are letters between emigrants and home, and petitions from small tenants to the landlord requesting various forms of assistance. The latter often define the terms on which the prospective migrant was prepared to depart. See for instance National Library of Scotland [hereafter NLS], Dep 313/1357, Petition of Alexander McKenzie of Clashnessie 8 January 1847 and similar references (for which I am grateful to Dr Malcolm Bangor-Jones).
7. See Eric Richards, *The Highland Clearances* rev edn (Edinburgh, 2008).
8. See *Report of the Commission of Inquiry into the Condition of Crofters and Cottars in the Highlands and Islands of Scotland* (1884), XXXI–XXXVI [hereafter Napier], q. 26956 and q. 26801.
9. McIver had himself thought of emigration to Australia as a young man, deterred by a lack of capital. See Evander Maciver, *Memoirs of a Highland Gentleman: Being the Reminiscences of Evander Maciver of Scourie,* edited by the Rev. George Henderson (Edinburgh, 1905), 32. Among his own large family there were several emigrants: he declared before the Napier Commission in 1883, 'I am the father of seven sons, and not one of these seven sons has remained with me. They went to India and Australia and Cape of Good Hope and to England; they went to fight their battle in the world, and I would recommend very strongly to the crofters of this country that their families should do the same.' When asked, 'But you would have liked to keep one son at home?' he replied, 'I would but I had no way for him. I could not afford to keep him at home'. *Napier* q. 26896–97. McIver's subsequent career is well documented in A. M. Tindley, 'The Sutherland Estate, 1860–1914' (University of Edinburgh, PhD thesis, 2006).
10. Famine was not new to the north-west coast. Sharp increases in mortality, disease and crop failures had been common even before the great augmentation of population in the late eighteenth century. See M. W. Flinn et al. (eds), *Scottish Population History* (Cambridge, 1977), 230–2, 239, and the *Statistical Account of Scotland 1791–1799* (East Ardsley, 1979), Vol. XVIII. The *New Statistical Account of Scotland* (Edinburgh, 1834–45) seemed to confirm Malthus' pessimism regarding the effects of emigration. Thus the population of Eddrachillis had increased from 941 in 1792 to 1965 in 1840, 'notwithstanding that many families emigrated', according to the Rev. George Tulloch. There was a similar increase in Assynt, but in Durness the population had not increased though it had been relocated and the minister believed that it could support three times its current population. In Assynt the population was reported to be in 'straitened circumstances', 'greatly overcrowded' and 'unless emigration on a large scale takes place, matters must soon come to a painful crisis.' In Durness there had been much unofficial subdivision among the small lotters which had led to early marriage and congestion. *New Statistical Account of Scotland* (1834–45) vol. XV, 95, 128, 113.
11. See, for instance, the writing of Donald Macleod in Douglas MacGowan, *The Stonemason* (Westport, CT, 2001).
12. See Richards, *Clearances*, 219.

13. Sutherland Collection, Stafford County Record Office [hereafter SC] D593P/22/1/: Stewart to duke, 11 May 1841. The principle was reinforced in the following years: McIver noted, 'I make it a rule that all Emigrants give up their houses to me to prevent them selling them, or admitting others into them.' McIver to Loch, 17 March 1848.
14. By August 1845 McIver had already ordered in supplies of meal from Aberdeen; the fishing had been very bountiful, and he was surprised at the number of 150 paupers in Assynt, which 'will cause a very heavy assessment – the number of idiots, blind and scrofulous people is quite surprising.' S.C., D593P/22/1/22: McIver to duke of Sutherland, 29 July 1845, 26 August 1845, 15 September 1845.
15. S.C., D593P/22/1/22: McIver to duke of Sutherland, 23 December 1845.
16. S.C., D593P/22/1/22: McIver to duke of Sutherland, 24 March 1846. The destitution test was applied on the Sutherland estate in conformity with the policies of the Destitution Committees in the south. See Devine, *Great Highland Famine*, 130 ff.
17. S.C., D593P/22/1/22: McIver to duke of Sutherland, 12 January 1847. Captain Elliott observed that a bounty of £2 was given by the duke to recruits in the 93rd regiment but 'homesickness prevents them taking it'. Captain Elliott, *Special Report on Sutherland and the West Highlands* (Edinburgh, 1848), 20. He observed, 'of the hundreds of fine young men fit for the Queen's service, not more that a round dozen have had the pluck to prefer it to lazy indigence and tobacco at home.'
18. McIver himself later testified to the bad feeling: 'the innate sense of wrong and injury by landlords, agents and sheep farmers towards small tenants appeared to fill the minds of many.' He attributed this to the removals which took place at the start of the century. Maciver, *Memoirs*, 62. On the earlier history of removals in the district see Malcolm Bangor-Jones, *The Assynt Clearances* (Dundee, 2001), and Malcolm Bangor-Jones, 'From Clanship to Crofting: Landownership, Economy and the Church in the Province of Strathnaver', in John R. Baldwin (ed.) *The Province of Strathnaver* (Edinburgh, 2000), 35–99.
19. S.C., D593P/22/1/22: McIver to duke of Sutherland, 18 August 1846.
20. S.C., D593P/22/1/22: McIver to duke of Sutherland, 25 August 1846.
21. Cf. Devine, *Great Highland Famine*, 92.
22. See the response of the duke to a petition from the inhabitants of Clyne, D593N/4/1/3: duke of Sutherland, 12 October 1846.
23. S.C., D593 K/1/3/40: Loch to the duke, 10 October 1846. Loch's philosophy of relief and emigration is reported in Eric Richards, *The Leviathan of Wealth: The Sutherland Fortune in the Industrial Revolution* (London, 1973), 216–18.
24. S.C., D593 K/1/3/40: Loch to Dundas, 1 November 1846.
25. S.C., D593 K/1/3/40: duke of Sutherland to Loch, 31 December 1846.
26. S.C., D593P/22/1/22: McIver to duke of Sutherland, 12 January 1847.
27. S.C., D593P/22/1/22: McIver to duke of Sutherland, 16 February 1847.
28. S.C., D593 P/22/1/22: McIver to duke of Sutherland, 2 March 1847.
29. S.C., D593P/22/1/22: McIver to duke of Sutherland, 29 January 1849.
30. McIver was repeatedly emphatic that the people needed to change their ways: 'idleness has been their ruin – and I hope the necessity of exertion which the failure of the Potatoes has occasioned will have the effect of making them all more sensible than have hitherto been of the evil effects of their indolence – indeed I am convinced much good is to follow the present crisis both to the people and to the Proprietors.' He saw the crisis in almost biblical terms, of famine leading to a form of moral redemption. S.C., D593P/22/1/22: McIver to duke of Sutherland, 5 February 1847.
31. S.C., D593P/22/1/22: McIver to duke of Sutherland, 23 March 1847.

32. McIver did not believe in the crofter system, old or new. As he later said, 'The crofter system has not within it the seeds of prosperity or of profit.' The extent to which McIver forcefully overturned the traditional quasi-communal foundations of the traditional life in Assynt was recollected in detail by the Rev. Dr David T. Masson. Maciver, *Memoirs*, 78, 293.
33. The duke also abated rents and supplied new seed potatoes to the small tenantry. The expenses were large and McIver commented: 'Your Grace will have to make large pecuniary sacrifices this year in supplying food to weak and helpless tenants who are unable to work and the Rents in general so low that it is easy for them to pay it – they seldom had more money than they have this year' – a consequence of good cattle and cheap prices and a good fishing season and the relative abundance of the employment supplied by the duke'. S.C., D593P/22/1/22: McIver to duke of Sutherland, 11 December 1846, 22 December 1846.
34. S.C., D593P/22/1/22: McIver to duke of Sutherland, 12 March 1847.
35. On temporary migration and its significance to the local economy, see Devine, *Great Highland Famine*, 165–6.
36. S.C., D593P/22/1/22: McIver to duke of Sutherland, 12 March 1847.
37. S.C., D593P/22/1/22: McIver to duke of Sutherland, 8 March 1847.
38. The prohibition of subdivision and the amalgamation of holdings were much reviled as an unnatural imposition by James Loch and the Sutherland estate. Devine, referring to Lewis, says that its population grew and remained in abject poverty precisely because subdivision was not controlled. Devine, *Great Highland Famine*, 223. McIver in 1883 testified to the extreme difficulty he experienced in checking subdivision. *Napier*, q. 26841.
39. S.C., D593P/22/1/22: McIver to duke of Sutherland, 10 October 1846.
40. S.C., D593P/22/1/22: McIver to duke of Sutherland, 11 January 1847.
41. There had been considerable emigration to Australia in the late 1830s which included that of William Stewart, the brother of the Scourie factor at that time, Alex Stewart. In 1841 he had returned on a visit and gave 'a very good character of such of the Sutherland men as he fell in with in the Colonies.' Stewart had been successful and was sailing his own ship back to Australia. Of the Sutherland emigrants he remarked, 'they are more industrious and better behaved than the other Highlanders who emigrated'. S.C., D593P/22/1/22: McIver to duke of Sutherland, 20 February 1841, 27 July 1841, but in early 1848 it was clear that 'None will go to Australia'. McIver to Loch, 17 March 1848.
42. S.C., D593P/22/1/22: McIver to duke of Sutherland, 23 March 1847. McIver described his approach: he told various communities of small tenants the terms of the duke's offer of assistance to emigrate and advised them to take advantage of the offer: 'at the same time ... I did not press them – that they were left to the freedom of their own will – and that as it was a serious step to ponder over for a day or two – and that all who wished to go should come here [Scourie] on Monday to enrol their names with the full particulars of the ages of their children ...' 26 March 1847. The cost of provisions was a substantial impediment to many of the prospective emigrants – again indicating that sheer poverty was a block on emigration. 8 March 1847.
43. McIver later reported that the duke spent £4,916 on sending people to America at their own request. *Napier*, q. 26841. He spent much larger sums on meal imports and job creation, some of which was recoverable in principle.
44. McIver to duke of Sutherland, 2 April 1847. DP593/P/22/1/22.
45. The problem of prospective emigrants changing their minds was not at all unique to the Highlanders. See for instance, Margaret Ray, 'Administering Emigration: Thomas

Frederick Elliot and Government-assisted Emigration to Australia, 1837–47,' *Australian Studies* 17 (2002), 40–1.
46. See, for instance, Devine, *Great Highland Famine*, 202.
47. S.C., D593P/22/1/22: McIver to duke of Sutherland, 23 June 1847.
48. S.C., D593P/22/1/22: McIver to duke of Sutherland, 28 May 1847, 2 June 1847.
49. The ordinary meal trade was inevitably disrupted by the intervention of the duke of Sutherland and other agencies; the traders were said to be 'afraid this year to import any'. S.C. D593P/22/1/22: McIver to duke of Sutherland, 5 February 1847.
50. S.C. D593P/22/1/22 duke of Sutherland to Rev. Gordon, 27 December 1847.
51. S.C., D593P/22/1/22 McIver to duke of Sutherland, 2 February 1848.
52. S.C., D593P/22/1/22 McIver to duke of Sutherland, 6 February 1848.
53. See Maciver, *Memoirs*, 216. He said that the people of Handa had begged to go to America: *Napier*, q. 26801.
54. S.C., D593P/22/1/22: McIver to duke of Sutherland, 19 May, 6 June 1848.
55. S.C., D593P/22/1/22: McIver to duke of Sutherland, 18 February 1848. In 1851 and 1852 the episode was repeated when the small tenants of Elphin successfully resisted an attempt to re-arrange their grazing and McIver implored the duke to reinforce his authority. S.C., D593P/22/1/22: McIver to duke of Sutherland, 14 May 1852. McIver described 'the very insolent spirit' of the people who were triumphant in the face of a weak-minded officer; it was all a terrible precedent as far as McIver was concerned. S.C., D593K/1/3/39: McIver to Loch, 4 April 1851; Fraser to Loch, 24 March 1851. On these attempted clearances see the popular recollection in *Napier*, q. 26955 and also q. 27480.
56. Captain Elliott RN, *Special Report on Sutherland and the West Highlands* (Edinburgh, 1848). McIver was delighted to hear that Elliott was to investigate the relief system: 'he will be amazed ... [by] the kindness and liberality exercised towards the small Tenants by your Grace' S.C., D593P/22/1/22 McIver to duke of Sutherland, 25 February 1848. McIver accompanied Elliott on his tour and explained the policy in detail, especially its priority to provide relief to the able bodied only in exchange for work, to economise and to prevent starvation. McIver was angered by petition which pleaded for free meal supplies. He regarded it as absurd and was deeply opposed to gratuitous assistance. They must combat the 'habitual sloth and indolence of character of our people' and seek their own regeneration. McIver was also concerned that Elliott meet the Free Church ministers 'for they are so mixed up with people's feelings and prejudices that all their statements must be listened to *cum nota*'. McIver to duke of Sutherland, 4 March 1848. On Elliott, see Devine, *Great Highland Famine*, 129–32.
57. Elliott, *Report*, 5.
58. Ibid. Elliott was also critical of their 'not accepting fishing opportunities, employment in the south or the army or emigration': 'They expressed considerable chagrin. Partly at their discomfiture, but also at the rather contemptible figure they cut under my rebuke.'
59. S.C., D593P/22/1/22 McIver to duke of Sutherland, 18 February 1848.
60. See Eric Richards, 'Varieties of Scottish emigration in the nineteenth century,' *Historical Studies* 21, no. 85 (1985), 486.
61. NLS Dep 313, Household and Personal, Box 41: Gunn to duke of Sutherland, 7 May 1848.
62. S.C., D593P/22/1/22: McIver to duke of Sutherland, 4 January 1849.
63. S.C., D593P/22/1/22: McIver to duke of Sutherland, 5 January 1849.

64. S.C., D593P/22/1/22: from New London PEI, Hector Falconer to McIver, 15 January 1849, McIver to duke of Sutherland, 5 January 1849. On the Poor Law and its implications for landlords, see Devine, *Great Highland Famine*, 207.
65. S.C., D593P/22/1/22: McIver to duke of Sutherland, 23 February 1849.
66. The duke was offering 'proportionate aid', about fifty shillings per person, which would cost him £750 though he was doubtful they would accept.
67. S.C., D593P/22/1/22: McIver to duke of Sutherland, 13 April 1849.
68. S.C., D593P/22/1/22: McIver to duke of Sutherland, 1 May 1849.
69. S.C., D593P/22/1/22: McIver to duke of Sutherland, 10 April 1849. George Gunn reported from the Dunrobin management that 'the Free Church Ministers are availing themselves of their influence in the Pulpit and in their daily intercourse, to dissuade the poor deluded people from leaving the country, but fortunately not with any great effect hitherto; their sinister object, to secure the continuance of a dense population around them, that they may more readily drain their pittance of wages, towards upholding of the Free Church, and more especially the Sustentation Fund.' NLS Dep 313, Household and Personal, Box 41: Gunn to duke of Sutherland, 7 May 1848.
70. See Bangor-Jones, *Assynt*; pace Devine, *Great Highland Famine*, 76.
71. S.C., D593P/22/1/22: McIver to duke of Sutherland, 5 April 1850.
72. S.C., D593P/22/1/22: McIver to duke of Sutherland, 5 April 1850.
73. S.C., D593P/22/1/22: Loch to the duke of Sutherland, 6 April 1850.
74. S.C., D593P/22/1/22: McIver to duke of Sutherland, 7 May 1850.
75. S.C. D593/K/1/5/70: McIver to duke of Sutherland, 5 April 1850.
76. S.C., D593P/22/1/22: McIver to duke of Sutherland, 7 May 1850.
77. On the rapid rise of emigration to Australia in 1852 to 1854 see Devine, *Great Highland Famine*, 198, 205, 254 ff.
78. S.C. D593/K/1/5/70: Loch to McIver, 14 April 1852.
79. S.C. D593/K/1/5/70: Loch to Sutherland, 9 March 1852.
80. There were concerted efforts to promote emigration from the Highlands to Australia in 1851–52. See *Emigration from the Highlands and Islands of Scotland to Australia* (London, 1852). In the initiating correspondence repeated reference was made to the problem of disentangling evictions from emigration in the current context. It was pointed out by Sherriff Fraser, for example, that emigration was 'a remedy that can not be applied by individual proprietors without giving rise to clamours and complaints of evictions that tend materially to render Highland property unpopular as an investment.' A public society for the purpose would combat the 'aversion to emigration and... the motives of the promoters disarmed. Ibid. 24. The Highland and Island Emigration Society eventually enabled the transit of 5,000 Highlanders to Australia in the years 1852 to 1855.
81. As we have seen, McIver certainly wanted to displace people still in the interior but was resisted effectively by the people, and restrained by the duke himself.
82. S.C. D593/K/1/5/70: Loch to McIver, 9 March 1852.
83. S.C. D593/K/1/5/70: Loch to Sutherland, 9 March 1852.
84. S.C. D593/K/1/5/40: Gunn to Loch, 12 April 1852.
85. S.C. D593/K/1/5/70: Horsburgh to Loch, 6 March 1853.
86. S.C. D593/K/1/5/70: Loch to W. A Loch, 2 June 1852.
87. S.C. D593/K/1/3/41: Horsburgh to Loch, 27 June 1853.
88. S.C. D593/K/1/5/70: Loch to McIver, 25 April 1852.

89. 1831 3161; 1841 3154; 1851 2989; 1861 3174; 1871 3003; 1881 2776; 1891 2536; 1901 2536; 1911 2111 ; 1921 1753. Devine assumes a natural rate of increase of 10% per decade, *Great Highland Famine*, 68, 70–3.
90. In the age group roughly 20 to 50 the female population was 55 per cent of the total. See also Devine, *Great Highland Famine,* 76.
91. By the 1840s the social structure had been polarised between the few large sheep farmers and the mass of the population. As the minister for Durness declared in 1834, 'The division of the parish into such extensive farms has ... depressed almost entirely the middle classes of society'. The estate managers acknowledged that the intermediate strata had been eliminated, leaving few natural leaders among the people, middling men who might have encouraged or deterred the will to emigrate. *New Statistical Account of Scotland* (1834–45), vol. 15, p. 102.
92. See Devine, *Great Highland Famine,* 68, 70, 76.
93. See *First Report from the Select Committee on Emigration, Scotland,* House of Commons, 1841; Sir John McNeill, *Report to the Board of Supervision: The Western Highlands and Islands* (Edinburgh, 1851).
94. See, for example, J. Mackenzie, *Letter to Lord John Russell on Sir John McNeill's Report to the Board of Supervision: The Western Highlands and Islands of Scotland* (Edinburgh, 1851).
95. *Napier,* e.g. evidence at Kinlochbervie, q. 26405–26593.
96. I am particularly grateful for the advice of Dr Robert Fitzsimons and Dr Malcolm Bangor-Jones, and that of the referees of this paper.

'I THOUGHT I WAS BACK IN AFRICA... AND DECIDED TO COME.' AN INTERVIEW WITH PROFESSOR JOHN D. HARGREAVES, HEAD OF HISTORY AT THE UNIVERSITY OF ABERDEEN, 1962–70[1]

TERRY BROTHERSTONE

I. Introductory

This is the story – a significant part of it at least – of John Hargreaves, Burnett-Fletcher Professor of History in the University of Aberdeen from 1962 until his retirement in 1985. It is both about him and largely told by him. Its wider significance is that it provides insights into the recent history of a United Kingdom university with a long and distinctively Scottish past as it confronted, first, the problems of expansion in an all-too-brief, optimistically democratic period in the Britain of the third quarter of the twentieth century; and second, the consequent difficulties of resource constraints in what Hargreaves as early as 1977 referred to as a 'financial ice age',[2] born of national economic crisis and then of a change in government policy to prioritise reducing personal taxation over sustaining public expenditure.

Hargreaves' birth in 1924 and upbringing was at Colne in Lancashire, in 'a secure Christian home, perhaps just a little too comfortably protected'.[3] A first-class history graduate of Manchester University, he arrived in Aberdeen with his wife Sheila to lecture in history in 1954. Eight years later he was appointed to the University's Burnett-Fletcher chair and the headship of the history department, performing the latter role until 1970. Between Manchester and Aberdeen he had spent two years at Fourah Bay College in Freetown, Sierra Leone, and his research interest in Africa was to lead to his becoming one of his generation's most distinguished historians of that continent. He played a key part in making Aberdeen for many years a major centre of African studies, and his intellectual engagement with Africa and its past informed his work in developing a history department in a growing university, not least in the way he promoted Scottish historical studies.

Latterly Hargreaves rounded off his years of multifaceted service to the University by collaborating with others in a quincentennial history project, which included – alongside a series of published volumes contributing to the growing field of university history – the creation of a body of oral documentation.[4] Hargreaves and his colleagues interviewed a range of people connected with the university, assembling one of the institution's major oral-history collections, second only to its *Lives in the* [UK North Sea] *Oil Industry (LOI)* archive.[5] Together they bear witness to the importance of oral history as a recognised and indispensable addition to academic research on the recent past. Some years ago, Hargreaves agreed to be interviewed himself, and, as one of the last of his appointees then still in post, and director of *LOI*, I was asked to conduct it.[6] This essay is based substantially on the corrected and archived transcript of the interview, which can also be checked against, and supplemented by, a personal memoir Hargreaves wrote at the turn of the century.[7]

This essay focuses on Hargreaves' early days in Aberdeen; on his professorial inaugural lecture; on the process of developing a history department fit for the expansionary 'Robbins years'; on the changing student body; on some of Hargreaves' ideas about African studies;[8] and on how his ideas about universities informed his attitudes in the troubled period when the university was caught up in the recurring funding crises that overtook the optimism of the 1960s. Underlying the essay – for which, despite its reliance on Hargreaves' testimony, I alone am responsible[9] – is my conviction that Aberdeen is a university with a strong, local identity, but that its unique characteristics enhance rather than limit the contribution study of it can make to the more general history of higher education in Scotland and the UK.

II. Coming to Aberdeen

The call that attracted the thirty-year-old Hargreaves to Aberdeen was not academic: indeed, it was not a human summons at all. Brought up in a Methodist family (though when he came to Aberdeen he had 'been received into the Anglican communion'),[10] he had completed his schooldays as a scholarship boy at Bootham, a Quaker school in York. He was only sixteen when he went to university in 1940, having rejected the school's suggestion that he should sit for an Oxford scholarship. Sixty years later, he reflected that, although a bright enough student, he would have lacked the maturity (or, one might speculate, the class confidence) to have survived in the socially elitist atmosphere of mid-century Oxford.[11] His interest in history had been inspired by an able Bootham teacher and by his awakening concerns about the immanent European war. Going early to university allowed him to begin on his degree before inevitable military service.[12]

At Manchester, the outstanding historian was Lewis Namier, who, after the war, supervised ('in a somewhat freestanding manner') Hargreaves' postgraduate MA thesis and appointed him to his first post.[13] A Christian socialist, Hargreaves was a member of the Labour Party. It was on general election night in 1950, when a group of canvassers gathered at his Manchester flat to listen to the results on the radio, that he met Sheila Wilks. They married later that year and, after the birth of the first of their four children (one of whom died in infancy), decided to spend a period overseas. Against Namier's advice – he and others thought it a disastrous career move – Hargreaves accepted the post in Sierra Leone.[14]

When the Hargreaves decided to return to the UK after two academically and politically instructive years, a provisional invitation from the University of Durham – which had links with Fourah Bay – seemed to suggest the family's likely destination. But Hargreaves, attracted to Scotland during short periods of army training, decided also to investigate a post advertised at Aberdeen. His visit to the grey-granite, regional capital of the north east was lightened by an invitation to Old Aberdeen from the University Secretary, W. S. Angus,[15] who provided him with dinner and an evening of indiscreet gossip. Aberdeen had begun to seem more attractive to the recently repatriated historian when, returning from near King's College to his city-centre hotel:

> I was standing outside the Old Aberdeen Town House, waiting for a bus [...] and suddenly there was a noise and a herd of cattle stampeded up St Machar Drive on the way to Kittybrewster [market]. I thought for a moment I was back in Africa! I was in a rather special place and it might be more interesting to work here than even in such a fine city as Durham! [...] [After consideration with Sheila and] seeing they were more generous than Durham had been in recognising what I had done in Africa, I decided to come [to Aberdeen] and see how I liked it.[16]

After some settling-in troubles, aggravated the first winter by inconvenient accommodation and illness, the Hargreaves did come to like it. They were to stay in north-east Scotland, moving first to a large house in the city's west end that, for some years, lacked central heating. Much later, after bringing up their family there, they moved to Deeside.

Aberdeen in the 1950s was 'a very different university from Manchester'. It was, Hargreaves recalled, very small:

> It was possible, indeed almost obligatory to make friends and have contacts in other departments and in the community of Old Aberdeen it was quite easy to do so. There was the little Senior Common Room in half of what is now the Elphinstone Rooms and there one met not only [...] other Arts colleagues, but made friends and contacts with scientists as well. [...] William Wightman, a Reader in History & Philosophy of Science [...] conducted a... I would call it an interdisciplinary group, which opened my eyes... but also over the first few years, not immediately [I got to know], people in [the] departments

of Economics, Politics and elsewhere with whom I had a lot to discuss and whom I was able to involve in guest lecturing in my course on modern British history.

In Sierra Leone Hargreaves had been able 'to spark off' a research community, but teaching had been his main role, as it was to be in Aberdeen:

> I had accepted that my main duty in Aberdeen, and probably wherever I was at that time, would be to teach. I had also begun research in Africa, which I wanted to continue, and which could be pursued in this country. It bore little relationship to the course I was immediately required to take, but so be it, I took my teaching seriously. I took my research seriously [too] and there was scope to do both and not too much time was taken up in filling up forms, reporting on what I had been doing and intended to do![17]

The Head of History and Hargreaves' predecessor as Burnet-Fletcher professor was the medievalist G. O. Sayles, a historian, said Hargreaves, who had achieved

> great distinction, whose scholarship was far beyond my scope to comprehend or criticise, and he was a congenial man, whose view was: 'I am hiring you because there is a gap in modern British history. I want you to fill it. I want to support you filling it with as much distinction as you can muster. But I don't particularly want to be bothered with your consulting me every few minutes.' [...] I was in charge of modern British history [...] [A]n assistant appointed at the same time as I was [...] worked with me as well as with the first year class, which George Sayles — in modern European history — retained the direction of.

Sayles headed a department of nine lecturing staff. As professor, he gave most of the lectures to the Ordinary (first-year) class which was devoted to European history. It met at the same time as Hargreaves' Advanced (second-year) class in British history, so his involvement with the first year was confined to helping with tutorial groups. The expertise of his colleagues allowed for teaching the medieval period, early modern British (including one honours course on a Scottish topic) and imperial and commonwealth history. Although, unlike other Scottish universities at the time, there was no separate Scottish history department, the first- and second-year (Ordinary and Advanced) classes in Scottish history occupied their own distinctive niche, taught by a historian from an older pedagogical tradition, a former Inspector of Schools, Walter Humphries.

Thinking about the University in the period before, as professor, he had 'a chance to do something about it', Hargreaves recalled:

> I was impressed by the care which the Faculty gave to what was then called staff/student relations. They had the Regent system, which, given the large number of ordinary degree students, was an attempt — into which, I think, most Faculty members entered very seriously at the time — to see that students

didn't miss out altogether in the gaps between the courses. That I think was a good feature of Aberdeen. [...] In the past, students had attended their seven courses over three years, and amassed their class certificates, and gone away with an array of class certificates. If they got — as many of them certainly did get — a *university* impression, it was largely formed outside the University, in the way that Robert Anderson has described in his study [of the student community].[18]

This meant that whereas normal course work would involve a student in 'discuss[ing] the English Civil War with one tutor, and he might discuss the novels of Jane Austen with another [and] he might do practical zoology with another', regenting provided the 'opportunity of interacting with a senior member on any wider scale than that'.[19]

The common room community that meant so much to Hargreaves intellectually was also important for someone coming to Aberdeen from outwith a city renowned, at least in popular myth, for its parochialism. The majority of the colleagues 'who frequented the Common Room'

were either not from Aberdeen or were not overly conscious of being *of* Aberdeen, if you take my point. It didn't really matter where you came from. I became conscious that there were those in the University who were less than wholeheartedly welcoming towards those from outside and certainly I became conscious as time went on, that in the city too, as we made Scottish friends quite easily, but a lot of them were either from further north or from further south by origin.[20]

As a university, thought Hargreaves, Aberdeen drew strength from its strong 'provincial' identity—it was a positive factor that 'was restrictive as well': 'by no stretch of the imagination, was it [or] could it be in the immediate future [...] a great cosmopolitan university.'[21]

It did, however, have an established international reputation to which Hargreaves contributed by taking up opportunities to work abroad. His determination, as he wrestled in his early years with keeping ahead of the students in his British history course, to develop research on Africa, pointed him in the direction of French colonialism as well as British, and also to the possibilities of looking at America from an Afro-American point of view:

There were [...] short visits to Paris, which were basically research visits and I was down in the archives, Monday to Friday at least. Then, in 1960, ... we went to [the USA, to] Schenectady. It was a small Liberal Arts college. It had a special relationship with St Andrews [University], and a colleague at St Andrews planted the seed that they might welcome an exchange with Aberdeen [...] [I] was beginning to get interested marginally in American history, particularly the history of black people in America, as a sort of offshoot from African history, and I thought this would be a interesting thing to do. So we did that. The exchange was arranged with a man [...] who taught here [in Aberdeen] for a year and subsequently became a very good friend. [...] Sayles saw [...] no objection. I don't think he was terribly thrilled, because of course he wasn't able to interview [my replacement] [...] but [that colleague] was a good scholar [...][22]

In teaching overseas Hargreaves was following the example of some pioneering colleagues in other departments: Aberdeen's provincialism did not mean that it lacked an international identity. It had a long history and in the 1950s boasted an array of scholars with a far-flung reputation, led by the Principal, Thomas Taylor, a lawyer who was 'a European figure'. As to Aberdeen's links with Africa, the history of which Hargreaves was later to examine in a monograph, there was 'Hamilton Fyfe [who] had been a considerable pioneer in university education' there'. In the university there 'was no sense that Aberdeen was a little place tucked away', although, when university expansion came in the 1960s, there *was* a 'southern English, an Oxbridge perspective' that had to be overcome, evidenced by, amongst other things by a Foreign Office seminar in 1970 which Hargreaves helped organise with a civil servant who was an Aberdeen graduate: 'quite a lot of ambassadors and Oxford dons came up and were quite astonished to find that we were not living as Eskimos!'[23]

III. The Chair and the Inaugural

The 1960s and 1970s in the UK were years when the professorial inaugural lecture flourished in an intellectual world which – at least in the humanities – has since been overtaken, not least by a bureaucratic, research-assessment culture that promotes short-term 'output targets' over strategic, critical reflection. Discipline-specific university departments headed by authoritative intellectual leaders, moreover, have given way to organisational models in which disparate groupings are subject to strategic plans with more of a managerial and financial than a philosophical rationale.[24] But that trend was unpredicted in 1962 and Hargreaves' inaugural fitted a well-established mould at the time. The lecture on 'Historical Study in Scotland' began by paying tribute to the new professor's predecessors, referred to the relatively short history of history-teaching at the University,[25] discussed historiography and the state of the discipline, and addressed the issues he wanted to confront as head of an evolving history department in an ancient Scottish university.

The Robbins Report was eagerly anticipated – the subsequently published version of the inaugural appeared in an issue of *Aberdeen University Review* that also carried responses to it – and it was well trailed that it would endorse a major expansion of higher education. A post-world-War-II generation of potential students had grown up with new aspirations. The Welfare State, set up by the Attlee Labour government in the 1940s, in support of which Hargreaves and his future wife had been canvassing in 1950, was part of a social settlement underpinning 'consensus' politics and informed with the idea that there could be gradual advance from electoral democracy towards social democracy and growing equality of both of opportunity and wealth. With state secondary school education reformed in the 1940s, a more educated and democratically-minded generation demanded enhanced opportunities for higher learning. The economic regeneration needed to sustain social development called for a growing cohort of intellectually critical and professionally trained citizens. Robbins was to make explicit the principle that a university education should be made available to 'everyone qualified and able to benefit from it', regardless of financial means.[26]

As a Fabian socialist and active member of the lecturers' union, the Association of University Teachers, John Hargreaves engaged in lively discussions about these issues, including the policies Aberdeen University should adopt. His period as Head of History was to coincide with the need to expand and develop the department to meet the challenges of the new period, when the – soon-to-be-disappointed – assumption was that growing numbers would be matched by commensurate resources. In the history of history-teaching at the University of Aberdeen this combination of circumstances gives Hargreaves a unique place. His inaugural did not specifically address the expansion of higher education but social and political awareness inform what he said. And he felt ready to focus his address on the importance of Scottish historical studies – not his area of expertise – in part because, in Freetown, he had grappled with the way in which he was teaching a native population about a history that had been done to them rather than *their* history.

The inaugural concluded by drawing together the threads of a learned historiographical survey, focusing on the future to which Hargreaves, from his African experience, thought a general history department in a Scottish university at a historical moment of political and intellectual transition could 'play an increasing part'.

> As historians of modern Scotland assess the work to be done, they ... should consider whether they might not ... return to what I have suggested is in origin an indigenous tradition of a broader interdisciplinary outlook ... [O]ur accounts of the development of Scottish industrial towns in the nineteenth century could gain greatly in depth if reviewed in the light which social anthropologists have thrown upon urban problems in contemporary Africa ... [emphasising] the strong links which normally persist between sections of the immigrant community and the rural community from which they came; [and] ... the interest and diversity of the voluntary associations which are so important in the transition to town life ... I hope we may use the tools of modern scholarship, not merely to destroy the legends of uncontrolled romanticism or to carry forward sterile disputes on points of national prestige, but to illuminate the historical significance and functions of distinctive features of Scottish society.[27]

The inaugural did not come easily. Interviewing Hargreaves, I asked if he had seen it as something of 'a missionary statement' by an Africanist who had been wrestling with teaching British history to Scottish students and who, as a Namierite, was aware of the need for students to understand the history of their discipline; or was it more 'a matter of getting something together'? He replied:

> Somewhere between the two I imagine! [...] I don't know if I would have said 'a missionary statement'. I remember the previous week I had not been feeling at all well and I had got these notes, and I forget if I got some sort of stimulant, maybe a bottle of whisky! But Sheila still remembers coming into the room — or somebody else coming into the room, saying, "He's tearing up his lecture!" I think I did this...[28]

It was not quite like that. Memory often emphasises the significance of an event at the expense of detail. Sheila Hargreaves remembered the weekend the lecture was being prepared more accurately. On the Saturday, John 'had had a bad attack of sinusitis giving him a severe headache.' When it persisted on the Sunday, she called 'our GP who was a near neighbour [...], and he provided some medication.' On the Monday morning – the lecture was to be at 5.15 – 'I went into the study & to my horror the lecture notes were being destroyed & a new version prepared.' The headache, however 'had gone & John never had sinusitis again.' The ingredients of the potion were never revealed, but something of the essence of the University of Aberdeen's local and international character is revealed in the revelation that the prescriber was a Dr Rice – father of C. Duncan Rice, a student in Hargreaves' department in the early 1960s, and a lecturer there from 1966 to 1970, who, after a career in university administration in the USA, returned to his *alma mater* in 1996 as Principal.[29] The inaugural, delivered headache-free, Sheila Hargreaves concluded, 'turned out very well'.[30] It did so, no doubt, because it was, as the story of its final hours of gestation brings out, the product of considerable agonising on what needed to be said. Half a century on, it looks pioneering.

Having been appointed to take charge of the core subject 'British History', Hargreaves was aware – as he had been in Africa in an analogous though not identical way – that the traditional syllabus and the materials available for teaching it were both anglocentric and permeated with whiggism. The latter approach – the idea that England's (now presented as Britain's) history of 'freedom', secured by parliamentary democracy, represented an ideal to which historians contributed by studying those aspects of the past that led towards this desirable and where-possible-to-be-emulated present – sat uneasily with much of the recorded experience of the Scots. The Scots, as Hargreaves pointed out in his lecture, had a long history of historical writing, but the twentieth century had brought a hiatus that only began to be overcome in the mid-1960s.[31] Politically Scottish opinion was still, at least on the surface, firmly unionist. Only in 1967 did the Scottish National Party win a fully-contested parliamentary seat for the first time.[32] The book Hugh Trevor Roper hailed as the first to make post-reformation Scotland comprehensible to a secular, non-Scottish scholarly community, Christopher Smout's *A History of the Scottish People*, did not appear until 1969.³³ The 'revolution'—as it has sometimes perhaps over-enthusiastically been called—in modern Scottish historiography lay in the future.

As Hargreaves remembered it, he became, as the 1950s wore on, more aware of the 'anomaly' of teaching anglocentric British history to Scots,

> and in a way it was almost a re-run of Sierra Leone, where there were courses... which had not given any recognition to the existence of African history in some respects... And of course there was a great shortage of books in so far as political history was concerned. There was a beginning of a... probably more than a beginning... a body of studies in Scottish economic and social history, and Henry Hamilton had of course been a great figure of this. [...] [He] had been a lecturer in [...] economic *history* and had become the Professor of Political Economy, while remaining essentially a historian. And Malcolm Gray joined that department in Aberdeen ... [working on the Highland clearances] [...] [a]nd much more [...] a very serious and valued colleague. So, in economic... well, if you like, fitting the Scottish experience into the industrial revolution story, however you told it, it was not too difficult. Politically, that was more so ... The only really serious modern book on the subject was by a lawyer, *Scottish Democracy* [... and] I devoured that. And I think that all I can say was that... — in lecturing, turning out the three lectures a week and in setting topics — when I got the opportunity to take in a Scottish dimension in readily accessible sources, whether they were biographical sources or whatever, I would do this. For example, for my Special Subject on Edwardian political history, I persuaded students to look at the *Scottish* election results of 1906 and 1910 which represented distinctive features, and you could relate these to some of the biographical materials and so on.³⁴

The influence of Namier was still a force, particularly the Namier whose detailed research on the eighteenth-century English parliament uncovered the importance of interest and patronage rather than ideas and principles.³⁵ It was possible, Hargreaves found, to encourage students to examine the idea that the politicians 'had been able to serve a sort of Scottish interest despite the mode of their election'—but this was more in the nature of a 'throwaway comment and sideline' rather than a systematic approach. And when he discussed with a young James Kellas, later a distinguished professor of Scottish politics and author of standard books on the political system, taking on the nineteenth-century Scottish Liberal Party as a postgraduate research topic, the greatest stumbling block for Kellas was the fear that, if he did, he 'would only get a job in a Scottish university'.³⁶

The following decades not only produced a substantial literature on Scottish history, based on expanding empirical research and beginning to engage with a wider historiographical agenda; they also saw increasingly intense public discussion about one of the questions Hargreaves alluded to in his lecture – the relationship of the Scots, their education system and their political system to their national history. These issues, rumbling in Scotland over many generations, became of more obvious social concern with the emergence of devolution as a major political theme in the 1970s and its accomplishment at the end of the century. The Hargreaves' inaugural, coming as perhaps it had to, from someone outside the intellectually somewhat old-fashioned world of 'Scottish history', anticipated the growing significance of this discussion.

The reception, less than acclamatory from Scottish history departments, was warm elsewhere, including 'a lot of very kind letters from other people in Scotland, and other people south of the border.' A former 'half-colleague' at Aberdeen, James Burns, 'who had been [...] — as [a political scientist] half in and out of the History Department' and was now pursuing a distinguished career in London, 'wrote a very long and appreciative letter'. When I suggested to Hargreaves that the lecture is 'one of the first public calls for a serious development of a scholarly Scottish history, certainly for the modern period'. he replied:

> I believe it is... apart from, 'what a shame our children don't know more about the history,' I think it probably is. There was a lot of that of course ... plenty of people saying, beginning to say, 'why do our children have to learn all this English history at school?' So in that sense there was an easy target to respond to. [...] I've forgotten the detail [... but the lecture] was discussed in the Historical Association [in Aberdeen].[37]

At Aberdeen University itself the longer-term outcome of Hargreaves' effort to put Scottish history into the historiographical mainstream was to be contradictory. A decade later, the attempt to find an innovating candidate to fill a chair of Scottish history, to which I return below, foundered; but a generation on a historian of Scotland, Allan Macinnes, became the first in the field to be appointed to the professorial headship of a general history department in an ancient Scottish university. By then, as Hargreaves acknowledged, many of the empirical gaps in the analysis of the country's past has been at least partially filled.[38]

IV. Making a History Department in the Robbins Years

When he became Burnett Fletcher Professor, Hargreaves identified a number of challenges:

> One, we were not strong on European history at all. The basic first-year course, for which I now became responsible, was European History, so we needed back-up in that. But, two, I had already [...] decided that we wanted to have

more Honours Options. I began to teach the Modern History of Tropical Africa [...]³⁹

He 'thought there had to be a different honours syllabus with a wider range, and this would involve new personnel'. The early appointments of his years as Head were aimed both at sustaining core courses and facilitating diversification. Qualified staff were not yet abundant (the Robbins-inspired increase in supply of able graduates seeking academic careers was some years off) and willingness to teach a wide range had to be balanced with the development of specialisms.

Two of Hargreaves' new colleagues had, like him, taught in Africa. Jennifer Carter not only took over British history but also became a key figure in university administration and, much later, a collaborator in the quincentennial university history project. Roy Bridges brought east African expertise to complement Hargreaves on the west and was to be a close collaborator in developing African studies. But he also taught European history, which was strengthened further by the appointment of a Russian, a French and, later, a German specialist.⁴⁰ The lead in Scottish history was gradually weaned away from Walter Humphries towards the research-based teaching of Donald Withrington who had been joined by the early 1970s by medieval, early modern and late-modern historians.⁴¹ A pre-existing post in American history was continued with a new appointment.⁴² British history was further acknowledged with the appointment of the Tudor economic historian Peter Ramsey to a second chair in 1965,⁴³ joining Doreen Milne who had arrived in 1950 teaching the early modern period. Expertise in the Mediterranean world added to the availability of Optional courses and developed not only the geographical and temporal span of the Department's offerings but also its interest in cultural as well more traditional approaches to the past.⁴⁴

A 'new syllabus came in',

> with the principle of Optionals introduced, and the formula was that there were four groups of Optionals [...] – the diversification principle was that there were four groups – one of which was American history on its own, one of which was a period of Scottish history. [...] The third one was non-Western history, in which Russia fell, Africa fell, and later [...] Mediterranean history fell; and the fourth one was an allied discipline which were approved courses from other departments.

A choice of Special Subject completed the new Honours offering. The reform was carried out on the basis of what was possible within Aberdeen's resources in terms of providing the most suitable possible coverage. Hargreaves himself had externally examined in Edinburgh so was aware of its situation but there was no formal consultation with other institutions in Scotland or elsewhere, far less external influence on what Hargreaves and his colleagues considered the way forward. It was an exhilarating period.

The department grew from the nine lecturing staff when Hargreaves arrived to eighteen when he handed over the headship in 1970, later to rise to more than twenty.

> I found it a very happy period. Very exciting. I don't think that's merely in retrospect. I was doing … it was exciting to build up the department. Departmental meetings became more interesting as time goes on! (*Slight laughter*) [...] [T]he student body had been I think improving for some time in numbers, and there had been a few extremely able students in the '50s [...][45] But [on at least two occasions] there were only as few as four students in the department doing Honours [...] [Of course it] meant that you had more time to spend with the four.[46] There had been some good students then, and some years which were a bit better than that [...][47] There was quite a lively year when I came back from the States, when we did my Special Subject on the partition of Africa [..][48]. But then … yes, it was very splendid. The first year in the chair was a year which I well remember [...]; and I think from that time onwards I was always conscious that there were a few students of real quality there and they are almost always in reasonable numbers. There were eleven students, I think, in that class and soon afterwards we are getting up towards twenty and thirty.[49]

The aspirations of a new type of leadership in Scottish historical studies announced in the inaugural suffered a setback in 1973 – one which came, symbolically at least, to have a broader significance in the University's history – when, following the appointments of the late 1960s, a chair in Scottish history was advertised. What followed, described by the department's historian as 'disappointment, even farce' and a 'minor *cause célèbre* in Scottish academic circles'[50] was remembered differently by Hargreaves. He agreed that the idea was an outcome of his inaugural but explained that initially, 'the reason it was frozen [...] was not because there was no money. It was because we failed to make an appointment when there *was* money'.[51]

The one internal candidate whom it 'might have been difficult to deny' was the medievalist, Leslie Macfarlane who had joined the department as an Assistant in 1953, and was ploughing his own, distinguished furrow with research that culminated in 1985 in a much-praised biography of the University's founder, Bishop Elphinstone,[52] Hargreaves recalled:

> I was clear in my mind, and I think it was probably shared by the rest of the committee that it would be preferable — unless we had a medievalist who was really star quality, and Leslie Macfarlane, interestingly enough, had not wanted to apply, he did not see himself as a Scottish historian [...] Leslie never wanted to see himself as a purely Scottish … as I never wanted to see myself as [simply] an African historian…

Hargreaves 'hoped to appoint somebody ... who would deal with the history of the modern – political/cultural history – of the modern period particularly, in a lively way.' The appointment board 'was not convinced that [any] candidate [...] would do this, and [decided] we had better leave it' for a few years:

> And I think that if we had been able to do that, I think that in four or five years, we would have had a much broader and more exciting field [...] I think it would [...] have gone to another generation. In '73 [...] there was no reason to anticipate the magnitude... I think it was before the oil crisis... there was no reason to anticipate that this would be a permanent freeze [...][53]

It was, for Hargreaves, important to fill the chair with a candidate with a new approach rather than simply 'to fly the flag for Scottish history'. The failure to appoint was 'a disappointment not a disaster'.[54]

In retrospect, however, the episode can be taken as foreshadowing the transition from expansion to retrenchment. Hargreaves' inaugural and the failure to create a new chair bookend one of the most exciting periods in the modern history of the University of Aberdeen, which is also intertwined with the wider history of British universities. It may not yet have been widely perceived, but the ship of the state that had sponsored the vision of the Robbins' report was already headed for the rocks.

V. Students

When Hargreaves came to Aberdeen in the 1950s, the student body was overwhelmingly local, in the geographically extensive sense that the vast majority of undergraduates came from Aberdeen, its hinterland and the Scottish Highlands. Compared to both Manchester and Freetown, Hargreaves, to begin with, found them

> [...] much more difficult to communicate [with] orally with than in either place. Intellectually, as regards serious purpose, and solidity of purpose [...] – if that's the right phrase – at the best, they were impressive. [...] [T]here clearly was an *Aberdeen* student. [...]

It was not until well into the years of expansion that the student body began to have a substantially more diverse geographical profile. But, as student radicalism grew internationally and nationally in the latter 1960s, Aberdeen, although not exactly a hotbed of protest, was not immune. In his memoir, Hargreaves highlights an anti-apartheid protest against the Springboks rugby tour in 1969, but that belongs a more general political story than that of 'student unrest' as such; and, interviewed, it was a relatively minor incident, reflecting the new self-confidence amongst students that first came to mind.

> I can't remember the background to it, but I remember a day when — I think I did it on my own, I don't think I asked anybody to join me — I would meet the students and take questions. I remember a confrontation with — now my very good friend — Jim Hunter, who was taking me to task about there not being enough Scottish history. Of course I had just appointed you to be our Scottish historian! [...] [I] tried to take all complaints seriously and I thought it was very good. It was very good that there was a bit of an eruption. I sometimes got cross with this and that...[55]

Hunter, in his own inaugural as Professor of History at the University of the Highlands and Islands Millennium Institute in 2006, was to recall:

> When I went to the University of Aberdeen in the 1960s, it was – though sadly it is no longer – a leading centre in the study of the history of Africa. And an Aberdeen course in African history, far more than course on the history of Scotland, shaped the way I think about the Highlands and Islands. But for my being taught something of Africa, for instance, I might not have come across that anti-colonial classic, Frantz Fanon's *Wretched of the Earth*. To this day, my yellowing paperback edition [...] falls open at the need [...] for colonised people to reclaim and reinterpret their own history [...]

The Highlands and Islands, Hunter acknowledged, 'were not colonised in the Africa manner', but that had not prevented his drawing on Fanon for the insight – gained from a student experience in which John Hargreaves with his own, as it were other-way-round, approach to the historiographical relationship between Africa and Scotland had played an important part – that 'a preliminary to progress [...] still consists [...] of challenging externally imposed, and almost always negative, interpretations of our past.'[56]

Within the university more generally, there were differences within the professoriate on the handling of unrest:

> [...] I think what was important was how Edward Wright handled it [...] He was by now Principal... [from] '62, the same time I became a professor [...] [having been] a [Mathematics] professor since the nineteen-thirties, and he was extremely good at consulting with SRC leaders and even those who had been elected as very 'Young Turks' — at taking their concerns seriously. There was a lot of concern about failure rates, I remember, and he set up research into that, and we did a little research in the department on our own account too. I think on the whole that period of student unrest wouldn't feature very prominently in UK-wide histories of student unrest in the '60s! But I think it was regarded as a basically salutary phase in the history of the University of Aberdeen [...] I think it was a tribute that the University could have it, and that it could take it. There were those who manifestly thought it was awful, that the students were getting above themselves [...] Maybe the University defused it all a bit too easily. I don't know.

A number of student occupations in the early 1970s were followed by another protest later in the decade over South African investments. But Hargreaves found, within the University, 'an emollient quality which has not been concerned to ignore and override student concerns, but take them on board and deal with them in a concrete manner.' All his comments on the relatively minor manifestations in Aberdeen of 'the student revolt' suggest that he looked upon it in a positive light, even that the University might have benefited from having to grapple with a more intense experience of it.[57]

VI. African Studies

This essay has concentrated on reporting Hargreaves' memories of his time as an Aberdeen University professor of history at an important historical moment, rather those of his role as an influential and pioneering African historian. A *Festschrift* which contains an academic memoir and a bibliography of Hargreaves' work by Roy Bridges has to be the starting point for the latter study.[58] But it is clear that Africa has been the focal point of Hargreaves' intellectual life not only in the sense that it was his chosen field of historical work, but also because his engagement with the continent has profoundly influenced the personal and political attitudes that informed his running of the history department and his influence over its aspirations. Hargreaves' hopes for the department and the difficulties encountered in trying to fulfil them were paralleled in the optimism that characterised African studies in the 1960s and the frustration that was the dominant mood of the 1980s. The turn to a 'financial ice age', the phrase coined by Hargreaves in 1977 in an article calling for universities, in adversity, to 'maintain broad horizons', could be applied generally but also to African studies in particular. At a conference on Aberdeen's history in 1992 Hargreaves was forthright in expressing the view that 'during the 1980s traditional humane values of higher education were hi-jacked.'

> Universities and colleges which saw their fundamental purpose as the advancement of learning and the education of students through the liberal arts and the diverse scientific disciplines which have grown out of them were increasingly required to justify their existence by financial criteria. The quality of learning came to be measured by its productivity.

Recognising the possible charge of elitism, he nonetheless made clear his own identification with the distress caused by this trend 'to teachers and scholars who believed education to be, literally, of priceless value.'[59]

This essay cannot deal with Hargreaves' large corpus contributing to African history but it should be reported that his personal narrative adds an important dimension to understanding his engagement with Africa and its history. We learn how accidental encounter, war experience and a political commitment to decolonisation contributed to that engagement.[60] How his experience at

Schenectady made him determined to return to Aberdeen and teach the partition of Africa rather than 'Edwardian Britain' as a Special Subject, in a period in Africa by then defined by Prime Minister Harold Macmillan as blown onwards by 'a wind of change'. How 1960 was a key year to be in the USA:

> it was the year America discovered Africa in a sense... The Kennedy administration and, ironically now, America's discovery of its own black population. The Black Muslims, the existence of the Black Muslims, although a Nigerian historian had done quite an interesting thesis on them already, but to most Americans, the first they knew of that was the demonstrations against the UN building. So 1960 was, both academically and politically, a crucial year for African studies.

How, in the field of African history, this was the beginning of what, in his memoir, Hargreaves calls 'the age of enthusiasm'. And how the Aberdeen University African Studies Group became a focus for interdisciplinary discourse at little cost, but great intellectual benefit, to the University.[61]

The 1960s and 1970s were 'the age of enthusiasm' because there was a belief 'that African studies could add to human knowledge in a number of fields, in social, environmental and historical studies; and also enthusiasm about the long-term future of Africa.' By the 1980s the political optimism and the academic interest – except, in the USA, at least partly for Cold War reasons, in southern Africa – had waned. And within African historical studies interest was shifting in ways which, Hargreaves was coming to think, required a different form of study from that in which he had played such a major role.

The point is best made here by quoting an exchange about a scholar Hargreaves came to admire greatly:

> [...] my ideal Africanist of this [later] period was my dear friend, Adrian Adams, who came to Aberdeen in about 1970 as a lecturer in Anthropology [...] not primarily in the first place as an Africanist, but as one who was more interested in anthropological theory – her PhD was on Lévi-Strauss [...] [She] hit on a research topic by chance on Senegalese migration, became deeply engrossed in its human aspects and the repercussions of the causes of migration, and finally made her home and her marriage within a particular community, cultivated the fields herself, and measured the housing, measured the agricultural holdings, was instrumental in reducing the Soninke language to writing for the first time and became a true Africanist – an Africanist of a very different sort, and a sort of which not many people could follow. So, as it were, the challenge of African studies was something it would not have been possible for me, at my age and in my circumstances, even if I had the abilities, to follow that particular line.

I interjected to ask if there was, for Hargreaves, a particular 'link between academic work and real life [...] between being involved with the people and yet having [...] detachment to write about them' that he saw 'as a kind of ideal, and one perhaps, in different circumstances' he might have liked to centre his life on.

> JH [...] I've always tried to maintain a foothold in [...] in the society about me. In [...] my early years in Sierra Leone, in fact I identified... I had attachments, rather strongly, to the African students, with their ideals and the splendid emerging African nation, and devoted some time to very amateur explorations in what passed for political science at the period, where they were being hopeful. So I have never felt detached from African life and I don't think I have ever felt detached from Scottish life in Scotland, as an immigrant in Scotland. And yes, I mean... I know I am not a candidate for sainthood (*laughter*) and I'm happy to leave my sins before the judgement throne, if you like. No, I've taken personal decisions at various times in my life, which have made this impossible.
>
> TB I'm not sure if I quite understood that train of thought exactly! All that about sinners and saints.
>
> JH Well, I am not quite sure what you're asking, but I would regard Adrian [Adams] — she was not a religious person — but I would regard her as a saint in the sense of a saintly person who took her great intellectual gifts into the service of a particular community and devoted herself to it with single-mindedness and that...[62]

At a seminar in the 1990s when Hargreaves had been working, self-reflexively, in the Fabian Colonial Bureau archives, on the period when he had first developed his interest in Africa, I had asked him to clarify what he had meant by saying something to the effect that the archives revealed that in going in an idealistic spirit to work in Africa, he and others were perhaps not doing quite what they thought they were doing. Knowing what the archives had now revealed, would he still have done the same? He had pondered before saying, 'Yes, on balance, I think I would!' And, in 2003, that 'would still be my answer. We work with foreshortened visions of our place in history, and do the best we can and I'm content for anyone who reads this interview and reads the memoir to make their own judgement [...]' I asked if his references to Adrian Adams reflected the thought that he could have had an alternative life, more immersed in African society in some way, which, in the 1950s would have meant greater political involvement. He replied:

> Yes, I think it would... Well, not necessarily in nationalist movements. I can think of academics, who spent many years in African universities without being signed-up members of [political movements]... particularly in West Africa. I can think on the other hand of Terry Ranger who worked in Rhodesia, where it was not possible... it was essential for him... if I had found myself there I would have hoped to have his courage in engaging in political activity. No, it is not missed political opportunities... There could have been another sort

of fulfilled life, but I would have had to sacrifice other things, personally and academically, in order pursue it.[63]

African studies, Hargreaves thought, were always likely to suffer 'when the academic world as a whole was under pressure.' In Aberdeen particularly the African Studies Group in which he had played a major role since its inception had depended on the appointments in departments like economics and sociology, and indeed history, where, as staff (including Hargreaves himself and later Bridges) moved on or retired, their replacement with Africanists became increasingly unlikely. He had regrets that the field so important to the intellectual ethos of the department he had developed should be more or less abandoned, but it was understandable. And, as a new century dawned, Hargreaves thought that, once again, 'the Africanist profession seems to be in not too bad shape'.

What, 'as a pioneer of the subject in British academic life', did Hargreaves think were 'the main achievements [...] in terms of how historians have contributed to understanding of African societies, and maybe even [in] politically beneficial effects'?

> I think [said Hargreaves] the main achievement — here, of course, one's talking of achievement in terms in western culture... it's a bit like the *discovery* of Lake Nyasa, which of course the Africans had known had been there all the time! African studies has revealed to the world, that what it previously thought of as a dark continent is not a dark continent. It is a continent of people with cultural aims of their own. It has removed any vestige of intellectual basis for a certain sort of racism. [And] this process of discovery [...] has enriched a number of disciplines [including] work on oral traditions, which [...] has affected the way oral traditions are being utilised by historians of other countries, and economists and sociologists and political scientists and anthropologists would all, I think, have something similar to say [...]

And as for the political future of Africa:

> The main ground for optimism is in the initiatives, which Africans are taking [...] [I]f you read the literature and never meet any Africans, you probably do tend to come out feeling pessimistic. [...] [W]hen I was latterly [external] examining over a number of years on two occasions in Freetown, reports on the university would not have indicated a very strong body, but I was extremely impressed by the way it was [...] maintaining university values. I would have great confidence in the future of communities like the village of Kounghani where Adrian [Adams] went to [live]. I only visited it once [...] but it was a visit which has enlarged my understanding of the word 'community', which we use so much in this country nowadays [...] So it is at that sort of level that I would remain in the long run, hopeful, optimistic about the future of Africa and Africans. That is not to give any prediction about the level of national income or achievement...[64]

VII. From Idea of the University to the Aberdeen History Department in Crisis

The contribution of the Hargreaves interview to university history includes a well-considered account of the role of a Scottish university dean – he served as Dean of the Aberdeen Arts Faculty from 1973 to 1976 – at a moment when the optimism generated by the relatively well-resourced expansion of the 1960s was turning to intimations of financial exigency. That can only be alluded to here, but the experience informed Hargreaves' early anticipation of the change to the 'ice age' and then attack in the 1980s on the values of humane learning. Although Hargreaves, after his Deanship, had had a productive year in Africa and had opted thereafter not to return to departmental administration when Peter Ramsey concluded his term (making way instead for Roy Bridges to become a non-professorial Head of History and the only one to date elected by his colleagues), he was fully engaged in discussions about responding to the cuts which soon became deep wounds.[65]

On a personal level the outcome was that, confronted with a reasonable early-retirement package that – if taken also by two other longstanding colleagues, as it was – would enable the History department to avoid the trauma, and the threat to academic freedom, involved in enforced staff disengagements, he decided to accept. Hargreaves served in the department part-time until 1985, whereafter his story is contextualised – apart from his involvement in the quincentennial history project – more by ongoing work in African studies and a growing active interest in the cultural life of the Deeside community whither Sheila and he had moved. But, collectively, when the University returned after what was then still meaningfully referred to as 'the long vacation' in 1981 to be confronted with a fully-worked template for across-the-board cuts, the History department responded vigorously and with its former Head's active involvement.

Of the initiatives proposed by the most active Association of University Teachers members in the Department – led by the distinguished Renaissance scholar, Judith Hook[66] – the one that Hargreaves became most involved in concerned the idea that revisiting the 'idea of the university' and its history should inform the campaign to combat the cuts or at least their worst potential effects. This brings the selection of extracts from the Hargreaves interview on which this essay is based to a suitable concluding theme.

At Manchester, recalled Hargreaves:

> I'd been associated with a group [...] which called itself the Moberly Group – basically they were concerned, I think, with democratising an elitist conception of the university and bringing it up to date, and making it a more vital part of culture. At the same time, as a member of the Labour Party, I was eager to see greater participation. There was the famous Kingsley Amis dictum – that 'more means worse' [...] [W]hen I came back from the States, I wrote a piece for the little [Association of University Teachers] house magazine [...] [on]

the merits and de-merits of a more open, not necessarily more democratic, but a much more open, university system. [...][67]

On taking on the headship of History in 1962, 'I had no doubts in my own mind that expansion from what we had nationally was desirable, I didn't need to wait for the *Robbins Report* to convince me of that.' But, concerned (as was Robbins) with the idea of what a university is, not simply with emerging political correctness of 'expansion', he was willing to engage with the 'most interesting personality' at Aberdeen to propound the Amis line – the nationally known Physics professor, and former adviser to Churchill's war cabinet, R. V. Jones.[68]

> Jones in the '50s was all in favour of expansion. He wanted to expand the Science Faculty, he wanted to extend his department. [...] He was very proud of the standard of the Physics department, in which he had had some very distinguished predecessors. He thought his students when he came to Aberdeen in '46 were a great lot. He [...] wanted to expand [...] into a major research establishment. When he discovered that not so many students of the same quality were coming forward, and that also that it was not so easy to have staff of a quality he wanted, he did a complete turn round and it was 'more means worse'! And there were long debates about that, and he made himself extremely unpopular. [...] I was one of the few people in the Arts Faculty who he would talk to [...][69]

Hargreaves' opposition to the cuts when they came, therefore, was based on reflection on the experience of a generation of intellectuals which had seen war service, had engaged with the establishment of the Welfare State and decolonisation, and had been involved with the debate about how a university system could, at the same time, remain a centre of critical intellectualism, academic freedom and educational standards and expand to meet the demands of a society of developing democratic opportunity. In much of this, of course, his story is far from unique. Yet it is a story that should repay attention from a generation of intellectuals and students increasingly remote from that experience and the optimism generated in the 1960s by the idea that higher education provided a key to a better society both in the advanced world and the post-colonial countries.

The University of Aberdeen, I suggested at the outset, can be studied both for its historical and geographical particularity and because that very particularity makes it a good vantage point from which to understand more general developments. From his memories of stampeding cows at King's College to his reflections on the evolution into the Thatcher years of the institution to which his working life has been largely devoted, Hargreaves, in the interview summarised here and in his personal memoir, contributes insights that, as I have tried to illustrate, can valuably inform the study of university history. In this lies the most basic (though far from the only) importance of oral history.[70] A major aim of this essay has been to draw attention to the existence not only of the John

Hargreaves interview, but also of a valuable archive of personal memories of the University of Aberdeen which he and others have compiled. The archive deserves growing attention from researchers.

Notes

1. This article started as an edited transcript presented as a documentary source. In response to an editorial request for it to be translated into essay format, I have selected themes and provided some minimal commentary and external referencing. But it remains essentially part of a self-narrated life story as that story relates to the narrator's career at the University of Aberdeen. As such it is an important source for the recent history of the University as that history was remembered on two particular days by one participant talking to another, but it should not be used without checking as a source for what are conventionally called 'facts'. The quotations used are from the transcript in the Aberdeen University Special Libraries and Archives (AUSLA). See AU MS 3620/1/127/1–3. Aberdeen University Oral History Interview with Prof. John Hargreaves, 2002–3. The interview was recorded by Terry Brotherstone in two sessions on 7 February 2002 and 27 March 2003 at the Hargreaves' Banchory home. It is cited below, with the permission of AUSLA as *Transcript*. I would like to thank John and Sheila Hargreaves for their hospitality then and on other occasions over many years.
2. John Hargreaves, 'Universities Must Maintain Broad Horizons', *The Times Higher Education Supplement*, 14 January 1977, 15.
3. John D. Hargreaves, *Attachments: an academic memoir* (unpublished mss, Banchory, 2000: available at AUSLA), 1. It cited with Prof. Hargreaves' permission. I thank the staff of AUSLA for their kindness in helping me complete this essay.
4. *Quincentennial Studies in the History of the University of Aberdeen*, a publication project first proposed by Hargreaves to the Senate in the late 1970s in anticipation of the celebration that culminated in 1995, takes the form, not of the traditional single- or multi-volume history of the university but of a series of fascicles listed on the University of Aberdeen University Library website. They include Hargreaves' *Academe and Empire: some overseas connections of Aberdeen University 1860–1970* (Aberdeen, 1994) and, edited with Angela Forbes, *Aberdeen University, 1945–1981: regional roles and national needs* (Aberdeen, 1989). The latter provides a researched context within which to read Hargreaves' remembered personal history. See also the volume by two leading participants in the quincentennial project, Jennifer J. Carter and Colin A. McLaren, *Crown and Gown 1495–1995: an illustrated history of the University of Aberdeen* (Aberdeen, 1994). The more general context is covered well by Robert Anderson, *British Universities: past and present* (London, 2006).
5. For the *Lives in the* [North Sea] *Oil Industry* archive, see Terry Brotherstone and Hugo Manson, 'North Sea Oil, its Narratives and its History: an archive of oral documentation and the making of contemporary Britain', *Northern Scotland*, vol. 27 (2007), 15–42.
6. I was Assistant Lecturer, then Lecturer, then Senior Lecturer in History from 1968 to 2008, and have been Director of *LOI* since 2000.
7. Hargreaves, *Attachments*.
8. On African studies and Hargreaves's contribution, see the expert essays in Roy C. Bridges (ed.), *Imperialism, Decolonization and Africa: studies presented to John D. Hargreaves with an academic memoir and bibliography* (Basingstoke and London, 2000).
9. The transcript on which it is based was corrected by Hargreaves, but neither he nor any of his closest colleagues have been consulted prior to the completion of this essay.
10. *Transcript*, 1, 42.

11. Ibid., 2.
12. Ibid.
13. Lewis Namier had been away during the War working for the Jewish Agency. Much of his writing on European history deals with the broad sweep of developments but his pioneering work on eighteenth-century British history, important for challenging the dominant, liberal-nationalistic Whig interpretation of the time, required so much attention to detail that, while an inspiration to Hargreaves – with his rather different political opinions – in inspiring empirical fastidiousness and integrity, it was not easily adapted to the task of teaching a general British history course. Hargreaves' memories of wrestling with this problem in 1950s Aberdeen make a historiographically interesting part of the interview. See below for Hargreaves' recollections of his lecturing on British history.
14. *Transcript*, 1, 3–4.
15. Angus had previously been Secretary to the University of Durham, the British university responsible for the validation of the academic work of Fourah Bay College.
16. *Transcript*, 1, 42.
17. Ibid., 3–4.
18. Ibid., 6. Robert Anderson, *The Student Community at Aberdeen 1860–1939* (Aberdeen, 1989) – one of the Quincentennial History studies.
19. *Transcript*, 6.
20. Ibid., 4.
21. Ibid.
22. Ibid., 7.
23. Ibid., 8.
24. As a measure of the intellectual impact of the changing culture, contrast Hargreaves' inaugural with the next Burnett-Fletcher lecture, 'A Strategy for History', given in May 1994 by the Scottish historian, Allan I. Macinnes, following his appointment as the sixth occupant of the chair (Hargreaves was the fourth). Macinnes paid due tribute to the Hargreaves' call for an international approach to Scottish history but adopted a much more managerial tone in promoting his own strategy for ensuring History's role in 'sustaining this university's standing as a centre of excellence – a premier league university in a premier league city.' See *Aberdeen University Review*, vol. LV, 4 (Autumn 1994), 350, 360. Macinnes' preface to Doreen Milne's history of the Department announced a new century dedicated to 'targeted excellence' – a goal Hargreaves might have endorsed, but a phrase he would have been unlikely to use: Doreen J. Milne, *A Century of History: the establishment and the first century of the Department of History in the University of Aberdeen* (Aberdeen, 1998), vi.
25. See Milne, *A Century of History*, esp. Chapters 3–5 and the Appendices, which provide important information on the growth of the Department over time and staff appointments and departures.
26. *Higher Education: report of the committee . . . under the chairmanship of Lord Robbins, 1961–63*, Cmnd 2154 (London, HMSO, 1963).
27. John D. Hargreaves, 'Historical Study in Scotland', *Aberdeen University Review*, vol. XL, no. 131 (Spring 1964), 250.
28. *Transcript*, 15.
29. For Principal Rice's tribute to Hargreaves, see Bridges, *Imperialism*, ix–x.
30. Sheila Hargreaves, letter to the author, 27 February 2009.
31. A. A. M. Duncan in *The Nation of the Scots and the Declaration of Arbroath* (London, 1970), 38, describes the first edition of Geoffrey Barrow's biography of Robert Bruce as 'the

first modern book on medieval Scottish history'; for the later modern period, William Ferguson, *Scotland Since 1689* (Edinburgh, 1968) was perhaps the beginning.
32. The SNP candidate won the Motherwell by-election in 1945 in an election during the 'wartime truce' between the main parties, losing it in the general election a few months later. Winifred Ewing's 1967 victory in the safe Labour seat of nearby Hamilton can be seen in retrospect as the real breakthrough in SNP history.
33. T. C. Smout, *A History of the Scottish People, 1560–1830* (London, 1969).
34. *Transcript*, 9. An anonymous reviewer points out that, although lecturing in constitutional law, Saunders was, by training, a historian who worked closely with historians and political scientists.
35. See footnote 13 above.
36. Kellas is Emeritus Professor of Politics at the University of Glasgow.
37. The reviewer points out that Gordon Donaldson's inaugural at Edinburgh – where however he held a *Scottish* history chair – raised some similar issues, though without the range of Hargreaves' references.
38. Hargreaves, *Attachments*, 46.
39. *Transcript*, 17. The growing strength of the Department was reflected in the publication of a more widely marketed text, R. C. Bridges, Paul Dukes, John Hargreaves and William Scott (eds), *Nations and Empires* (London, 1969).
40. Paul Dukes, William Scott and John Hiden.
41. Grant Simpson, David Stevenson and Terry Brotherstone.
42. Edward Ranson.
43. For my obituary of Ramsey, see *Aberdeen University Review*, vol. LXII, 1 (Autumn 2008), 89.
44. Ann Williams, Judith Hook (see note 67 below).
45. The subsequently prolific Scottish historian Bruce Lenman was one.
46. The two years with four were actually 1960 and 1961. Milne, *A Century of History*, 95.
47. One year included Kellas and Nicholas Phillipson, the most recent biographer of Adam Smith.
48. Tom Barron became a lecturer in Imperial history at Edinburgh; David Ross went on to teach African history at Simon Fraser University in Canada.
49. *Transcript*, 18. Hargreaves recalled Duncan Rice, Allan McLaren and Ian McCalman as amongst the particularly able students.
50. Milne, *A Century*, 78.
51. *Transcript*, 24. On the Scottish chair, see too *Attachments*, Chapter 7. The failure to create the chair marks the end of the expansionary period only in a symbolic sense. Even at the end of his Faculty of Arts Deanship in 1976, Hargreaves was only dimly perceiving the crisis ahead.
52. Leslie J. Macfarlane, *William Elphinstone and the Kingdom of Scotland, 1431–1514* (Aberdeen, 1985).
53. *Transcript*, 25.
54. Ibid., 30–1.
55. Ibid., 20.
56. James Hunter, 'History: its key place in the future of the Highlands and Islands', *Northern Scotland*, vol. 27 (2007), 6–7.
57. *Transcript*, 21–2. Anderson, *Student Community*, 118, confirms that 'it would seem that the conservative patterns of student life' discernable up to 1939 'persisted until at least the

1960s, but that since then there have been global changes in youth culture and generational attitudes.'
58. Bridges, *Imperialism*. See too Roy C. Bridges (ed.), *An African Miscellany for John Hargreaves* (Aberdeen, 1983), published by the Aberdeen University African Studies Group.
59. John Hargreaves, 'The Added Values of Learning', in Terry Brotherstone and Donald J. Withrington (eds), *The City and its Worlds: aspects of Aberdeen's history since 1794* (Glasgow, 1996), 82–3.
60. *Transcript, passim*.
61. On the African Studies Group see Hargreaves, *Attachments*; Bridges, *Imperialism*; and Bridges, *African Miscellany*.
62. *Transcript,* 39–40. Since this interview, Hargreaves has published *Adrian Adams in Kounghani: a memoir with letters* (Banchory, 2005).
63. *Transcript,* 40. Terence Ranger, historian of Zimbabwe, emeritus fellow of St Antony's College, Oxford, formerly Rhodes Professor of Race Relations, co-founder of the Britain Zimbabwe Society.
64. *Transcript,* 41–2.
65. *Transcript,* 40–1.
66. Hargreaves' obituary for Hook appeared in *The Times*, 3 August 1984. For a contemporaneous and related initiative at the time, see Terry Brotherstone and Judith Hook (eds), *Universities Against the Cuts* (Aberdeen Association of University Teachers, 1982).
67. Walter H. Moberly, a former Vice-Chancellor of Manchester University, Chairman of the University Grants Committee, 1935–49, created national interest with his Student Christian Movement pamphlet, *The Crisis in the University* (London, 1949).
68. Hargreaves' interview with Reginald V. Jones is in the University of Aberdeen Oral History collection.
69. *Transcript,* 12.
70. See on this, as a starting point, Alessandro Portelli, 'What Makes Oral History Different?', in Robert Perks and Alistair Thomson (eds), *The Oral History Reader* (Abingdon, 2nd edn, 2006), 32–42.

CORRESPONDENCE

POMEGRANATES, OPIUM AND POPPYCOCK

In illustrating disagreeable aspects of Scotland's global impact, Ewen Cameron cites the gateposts of Alexander Matheson's Ardross House – 'adorned with representations of poppies' – as evidence of his lack of reticence 'about his connections with the opium trade'.[1] He follows other historians in this erroneous identification and in using it to illustrate the valid grander point; he further suggests, without foundation, that 'a later owner of the house had these altered to resemble pomegranates'.[2] An example of public acknowledgement of the family's opium-related wealth is available at another location nearby.

The initial error is easily made as the pods held by the gate-post dogs bear a resemblance to opium poppy heads.[3] Their size and shape, their leaves and large seeds, however, clearly identify them as pomegranates. This is attested by the record. The castle was built in 1880–1 during Alexander Matheson's time by Alexander Ross, as a Victorian Scots baronial mansion – incorporating parts of an earlier home. It was sold in 1898 by his son Sir Kenneth Matheson to Charles William Dyson Perrins (1864–1958), who added the portcochere and the billiard room, and added the family's distinguishable coat-of-arms to the north entrance as well as the octagonal gate piers.[4]

The said coat-of-arms of Dyson Perrins, millionaire grandson of the co-founder of Lea and Perrins Worcestershire Sauce, incorporates a talbot hound holding a slipped pomegranate, with three further pomegranates in the shield. The crest appears on each side of the portcochere, on the gate posts and on the castle's stained glass windows – also added by Perrins.[5] Cameron points out that the Matheson family 'did not make its fortune by trading in pomegranates'. Nor indeed did Perrins (they are not part of the Worcestershire sauce original ingredients); pomegranates, however, are not uncommon in heraldry.

The Matheson opium connection is publicly attested in the mausoleum of Sir James Matheson (1796–1878), Alexander's uncle and co-founder of Jardine Matheson & Co. Here in the Lairg cemetery, the capitals of eight Corinthian columns display, on each side, sprays of three opium poppy seed heads.[5] We can assume that these were to a design sanctioned by Sir James himself, or at least by his widow. In making the point about the Highland opium connection and brazen acknowledgement thereof, it is important to do justice to local historical detail.

Adrian Clark
DOI: 10.3366/nor.2011.0007

Notes

1. Ewen Cameron, 'Scotland's Global Impact', *Northern Scotland*, new series, 1 (2010), 9–11.
2. Norman Newton, *The Life and Times of Inverness* (Edinburgh, 1996), 125; John Keay and Julia Keay, *Collins Encyclopaedia of Scotland* (London, 1994), 558. Correctly identified by David Alston in *Ross and Cromarty, A Historical Guide* (Edinburgh, 1999), Plate 16.
3. Incorrectly referred to by Keay, *Collins Encyclopaedia*, as griffins.
4. Historic Scotland Listed Building Record.
5. Historic Scotland quotes Groome's *Ordnance Gazetteer of Scotland* (1885), 451: '6 Corinthian columns with poppy seed heads decorating capitals'. There are in fact eight columns.

REJOINDER TO PROFESSOR CAIRNS CRAIG

To paraphrase Blackie's 'sincere admirer' Oscar Wilde, one bad notice may be regarded as a misfortune, but two from the same reviewer looks like carelessness. Cairns Craig in the *Scottish Historical Review* October 2008, and again in *Northern Scotland* May 2010, has decided *John Stuart Blackie* is a book in which the author 'misses few opportunities to undermine his subject's importance and achievements'. None of the dozen reviewers in other journals has detected a 'tone of condescension' in my treatment of Blackie, and aspects of his life which Craig finds interesting (university reform, charismatic teaching, Gaelic, crofters' rights, Scottish devolution) are all in the book. What then is the problem? That I have 'prejudged' Blackie 'rather than leaving such judgements to . . . readers', and that I have treated him as a 'conundrum'. Blackie's life is a conundrum only in the sense that any life is. 'Condescension' occurs when the biographer, or reviewer, suggests otherwise.

On what George Davie called the 'provincialisation' of Scotland after 1843, there is debate. Blackie regarded the charge of heresy against Robertson Smith in 1878 as a repeat of attempts to deprive him of his chair in 1839. Blackie won, but Smith spent the last thirteen years of his life outside Aberdeen, eleven of them productively in Cambridge. Religious sectarianism (even after the 1853 Act) and meagre government funding affected the development of Scottish intellectual life, concentrated in its universities. Glasgow's new Gilmorehill buildings (1870) had no laboratory space, and at Edinburgh science competed with the powerful Medical School. Clerk Maxwell was a Marischal professor for four years, a

London one for eleven, and a Cambridge one for eight, founding the Cavendish Laboratories. Frazer was a Cambridge fellow, from his early twenties. Kelvin, Bain, Masson and Tait returned to Scotland, but outward migration also had a positive role.

Stuart Wallace
DOI: 10.3366/nor.2011.0008

BOOK REVIEWS

Land, Law and People in Medieval Scotland.
By Cynthia J. Neville. Pp. viii, 256.
ISBN 9780748639588 (hbk).
Edinburgh: Edinburgh University Press, 2010. £60.00.
DOI: 10.3366/nor.2011.0009

The historiography of medieval Scotland is often focused most on those at the peak of the social scale. Contemporary kings, lords and nobles, involved as they were in the acquisition of territory and the governance of men, have left the largest imprint in extant record sources. For the period of growing 'Norman' and continental influence in Scotland from the twelfth to the fourteenth century, it has been possible to utilise these sources to track the development of European-style lordship in the Scottish political landscape. Less analysis has, however, been possible on the impact of that change on the people of Scotland and less still on the people of those 'Gaelic' areas where the same continental influences took longer to find widespread acceptance. The change that affected the whole kingdom during the 'Anglo-Norman era', from the elites to the serfs, both Highland and Lowland, remains in need of modern and more complete examination. Neville's book is a laudable attempt to provide such a study.

The book begins with examination of the baronial courts of medieval Scotland, where all three elements of the title were brought together as the lord passed judgement on territorial and familial issues. The assembly of local worthies to discuss and, most importantly, to witness the decision or declaration of the lord was a vital element of the ceremony of the court, especially in those areas where the importance of written testimony was slower to develop. The decisions of the baronial court were vital to the daily lives both of those who possessed title to the land, and to those who worked on it.

Territorial matters are further examined in the second chapter with discussion of perambulation of the land as a means of measuring out and confirming the extent of newly acquired or granted lands. The importance of physically walking the boundaries of such territory was vital in a period when incoming lords and landholders were first asserting their rights over what was truly theirs. In a society conscious of its duty to provide for future generations, the recognition of those boundaries – written down in detailed charter clauses, represented in the landscape by various markers, or personally witnessed and remembered by trusted members of the community – ensured that arguments over possession of territories would not usually end up before those same baronial courts that are discussed in chapter one. The spread of perambulation as a standard element of the process of land granting, and the zealous way in which ecclesiastical benefactors in particular protected the boundaries of their territory, go a long way towards reinforcing the importance of land to those who possessed it, and the lengths pursued to ensure continued ownership.

Completing the section on 'Land and Law', the third chapter discusses the progression of the business of territorial transaction from a system in which the oral testimony of local dignitaries was sufficient proof of the deed, to the physical commemoration of the act in the production of a written and sealed document. Concurrently with this the chapter explores the power of the written word, and the extent to which the 'trust in writing' that is represented in the surviving charters and brieves of the period took hold as an alternative to oral testimony. This progress is important in the kingdom as a whole, representing as it does the more ready acceptance of continental-style practice in the production of formal written grants relating to territorial acquisition. It is especially important in those 'Gaelic' areas of the kingdom where, as Neville explains, written documents and the seals that validated them continued to represent a somewhat alien element. Although 'Gaelic' lords often utilised seals and written charters to their own advantage – and in some cases in order to satisfy the needs of lowland ecclesiastical beneficiaries of territorial grants – there remained the possibility of retaining older traditions. 'Gaelic' nobles could continue to depict their own and their family's power and influence without recourse to Latin inscriptions and heraldic symbols.

The book's second section, dealing with 'Land and People', begins with a case study of the earls of Strathearn and their possessions in Northumberland acquired from marriage with the Muschamp family. Representing as it does the territorial aggrandisement of a 'Gaelic' noble by acquisition of rich northern English territories, this case study presents an interesting example of cross-border landholding in the years before the outbreak of the Wars of Independence made such possessions impossible. The acquisition of the estate by Nicholas Graham, as a result of his marriage to Mary of Strathearn, demonstrates the means by which contemporary nobles sought to build political alliances with other important families. The period of Graham possession of the Muschamp inheritance deals with the time that has proved most fertile for historians of Scottish lordship, namely when loyalties were divided by the beginning of Anglo-Scottish warfare and decisions had to be made over which territories were more important to those involved. The split in the extended family that saw Mary Graham live out the remainder of her life on her English estate, far from her Strathearn birthplace, is indicative of the change in landholding brought about by the Scottish Wars of Independence.

The relationship between the land and those at the lowest end of the social spectrum is the focus of the fifth chapter. The experience of peasants and serfs, free and unfree, is difficult to extract from existing materials and Neville makes a case for examining Irish documents to find similar trends to those found in Scotland. Although this comparative element is useful in the overall examination of the unfree, it remains impressive to find that careful examination of extant records does still provide insight into Scottish treatment of such people and their extended families. That serfs continued to be exchanged as part of territorial transactions into the fourteenth century – with the church a particular beneficiary as it sought labour to work its vast estates – is of particular interest considering contemporary religious views of slavery.

In rounding off the work Neville returns to her close examination of charter evidence for examples of the 'language of friendship' in medieval documents and the meanings that lay behind the use of such terminology. The development of standard clerical rhetoric is undeniably part of the process that led to such references being made, but the author is surely correct in asserting that the language employed also helped to form or emphasise ties of family, loyalty and friendship that were essential to political relationships of the period.

It is those relationships – crossing at times social, cultural or geographical boundaries – that emerge most clearly in Neville's work. She has constructed a study based firmly on the fundamentals of contemporary record evidence, exploring in detail the development of legal and territorial organisation in medieval Scotland and the impact that such change and later consolidation had on the people of the whole kingdom. The two parts of this comprehensive work – discussing in turn 'land and law' and 'land and people' – scrutinise in particular the nature of change in medieval Scotland and its impact on all matters of life in the contemporary kingdom. Notably, it takes the opportunity to compare and contrast the experience of 'Gaelic' landowners and their tenants as they dealt with the seismic changes in seigneurial practice taking place during this period. As a result, the developments and changes of the 'Anglo-Norman era' emerge in stark relief, and the reader is provided with a fascinating account not just of 'what happened', but of how the spread of continental influences took hold in Scotland as well as the impact of these influences on medieval Scots.

Iain MacInnes
Centre for History, University of the Highlands and Islands

Life on the Edge: The Cistercian Abbey of Balmerino, Fife (Scotland).
Cîteaux: Commentarii Cistercienses, 59 (2008), parts 1 and 2 (2009).
Edited by Terryl N. Kinder. Pp.168; 35 colour illustrations.
ISBN 9782960064711 (pbk).
Forges-Chimay, Belgium, 2008 (dist. by Oxbow, Oxford). £20.00.
DOI: 10.3366/nor.2011.0010

Life on the Edge is a collection of essays that re-examines the surviving documentary and physical evidence for the Cistercian abbey of Balmerino and provides essential reading for all those interested in this small Scottish house. The book explicitly forms part of a more recent movement in Scottish monastic studies spearheaded by one of the contributors, Richard Oram, to explore the relationship between the community, the estates that supported it, and the social and geographical landscape in which it operated. The articles offer an interdisciplinary approach to the subject matter and, with the exception of the final piece, show how the analysis of even fragmentary evidence can offer significant insights into different aspects of Balmerino's history.

Matthew Hammond's article provides a fitting start to the book by focusing on the foundation of the abbey and its early years. His study rests largely on charter evidence, which is neatly tabulated and provides clear support for his argument concerning the changing relationship of the house with one of its patron saints, Edward the Confessor. The unusual choice of St Edward as patron of both a Cistercian and Scottish house reflected the influence of Queen Ermengarde (d. 1233) who is shown to be the driving force behind the foundation of Balmerino in 1229. Hammond discusses the reasons for Ermengarde's personal devotion to the saint and argues that the association of Edward with the new foundation represented 'a wisely-chosen intercessor to help the young English wife of the Scottish king to conceive an heir to the kingdom' (15). Although Hammond's emphasis on Edward's appeal as an intercessor offers a welcome foray into the wider religious context of the foundation, the choice of Edward as patron for a fruitful royal union seems somewhat strange considering the king's own failure to produce offspring and it is disappointing that this aspect of the saint's character is not accounted for in what is otherwise a persuasive analysis.

In the second essay Julie Kerr turns our attention to a generally later period of Balmerino's history with much of the evidence cited dating to the fifteenth and sixteenth centuries. Although Kerr admits that the surviving sources are 'scant and fragmented' (37), she provides a number of detailed examples that offer glimpses into the social context of monastic life, from family background to the involvement of individual monks in political and ecclesiastical affairs – the discussion concerning Abbot Walter Bunch provides a particularly detailed case study. The article passes a glancing spotlight over various individuals and incidents in Balmerino's history and, as with any survey of this kind, raises more questions than it answers. However, in so doing, it highlights the rich detail and research possibilities to be found in this kind of material.

Richard Oram's essay investigates another aspect of Balmerino's history. By comparing the early grants to the community with evidence for the abbey's landholdings that survive in sixteenth- and seventeenth-century documents, his article evaluates the economic viability of Balmerino's original endowment. The earliest properties granted to Balmerino consisted largely of arable land, the majority of which seem to have been cultivated by monastic tenants rather than by the monks themselves, and reflects the community's entry into an already heavily colonised agricultural landscape. The grazing of flocks on upland properties and coastal possessions allowed Balmerino to become a minor player in the Scottish wooltrade, while the commercial operation of fisheries on the Tay seems to have been another profitable part of the abbey's economic portfolio. But it seems that this profit did not amount to much. Oram interprets the tenacity with which the monks both held onto their original endowment and defended their most lucrative possessions as an indicator of the precarious nature of the abbey's finances. As this detailed study concludes, despite its royal founders, Balmerino operated more as a small aristocratic foundation that simply 'could not afford to permit any unchallenged erosion of their interests' (79).

The final three articles of the collection assess the architectural, toponymic and (what would be) archaeological evidence associated with the house. The fourth essay allows Richard Fawcett to cast his expert eye over the extant remains of Balmerino's abbey buildings. He compares the possible layout of the abbey with other Scottish houses of similar date and stature, and makes some insightful comments on the structural process of building. As with the other articles in this collection, Fawcett's commentary is well illustrated, although the colour quality of some of his photographs has suffered at some point in the publication process. In the penultimate essay, Gilbert Márkus presents a toponymic analysis of the landscape around Balmerino from the ninth to the sixteenth centuries. His article traces the evolution of place names in various documents and maps, organised according to the religious community whose ownership shaped them. Márkus concludes that at the time of Balmerino's foundation in the early thirteenth century the area around the abbey was still populated largely by Gaels with only a minor Scots presence – and it is a shame that a hint of this conclusion is not provided earlier in the essay since it would allow readers to appreciate more fully the significance of the evidence being presented.

The final tantalising contribution to this collection is a very brief piece by Piers Dixon outlining the new LiDAR survey of Balmerino Abbey and its hamlet being undertaken by RCAHMS and the University of Cambridge. Unfortunately, since Dixon provides only a small sample of data from the survey – presumably this information is either still being processed or is being published elsewhere – the most important contribution of this essay is the two recent aerial photographs of the site. In contrast to the detailed articles that go before it, Dixon's succinct research statement is a disappointing finale for this fine little collection. However, it does at least show that the message of this book, that important insights can be gained from research into seemingly obscure, poorly documented monastic houses, is being both heard and acted upon.

Helen Birkett
Medieval Studies, University of York

Scottish Highlanders and Native Americans: Indigenous Education in the Eighteenth-Century Atlantic World.
By Margaret Connell Szasz.
ISBN 9780806138619 (hbk).
Norman: University of Oklahoma Press, 2007. £34.95.
DOI: 10.3366/nor.2011.0011

White People, Indians and Highlanders: Tribal Peoples and Colonial Encounters in Scotland and America.
By Colin G. Calloway. Pp. xxi, 368.
ISBN 9780195340129 (hbk).
Oxford: Oxford University Press, 2008. £22.50.
DOI: 10.3366/nor.2011.0011

Long ago, when researching my PhD thesis about the evolution of crofting, it began to be apparent to me, as I tried to come to grips with the nature of pre-clearance society in the Gaelic-speaking Highlands and Islands, that my undergraduate study of Scottish and British history was of much less use as an aid to understanding this society, and to gaining some insight into the character of the external forces operating on it, than was a course I had taken on the history of sub-Saharan Africa. The Highlands and Islands, to be sure, were not colonised in the way that Africa was colonised. But in both areas long-established social and cultural norms, deriving in the Highlands and Islands every bit as much as in Africa from the primacy of kinship, were subverted or shattered as a result of formerly autonomous or semi-autonomous localities being drawn more and more into the ambit of the commercial and industrial civilisation which took shape in England and in Lowland Scotland during the seventeenth and eighteenth centuries. While I appreciate that not everyone is convinced of the validity of this perspective, it is one I have stuck with – not least because of its usefulness. When grappling with the impact on the Highlands and Islands of initiatives like James VI's planting of the so-called Fife Adventurers in Lewis, or when assessing the effects of the land management policies associated with Patrick Sellar, James Loch and other early nineteenth-century 'improvers', it is – at the minimum – helpful to draw on the insights to be gained from the notion that people living in the Highlands and Islands between, say, 1500 and 1850 were experiencing much the same sort of transformational upheavals as were experienced, at the same time or later, by lots of other people in lots of other places.

One such place was North America. Here, starting in the seventeenth century, Indian peoples, whose tribes shared many characteristics with Scotland's Gaelic-speaking clans, found themselves dealing with expansionary forces akin – indeed arguably identical – to those then reshaping the Highlands and Islands. Now two American historians, Colin G. Calloway and Margaret Connell Szasz, both of them knowledgeable about the Native American past, have set out to examine the extent to which it is possible to illuminate the Native American experience on the one hand, and the Highlands and Islands experience on the other, by first comparing them and then by exploring links between them.

Szasz's starting point is the work of the Society in Scotland for the Propagation of Christian Knowledge (SSPCK), which was founded in Edinburgh at the start of the eighteenth century with a view to bringing civilisation and presbyterianism (overlapping concepts as far as the SSPCK was concerned) to the many Highlanders who knew no English (which the SSPCK thought bad) and who inclined to espiscopacy, catholicism and Jacobitism (which the Society thought even worse). Throughout its crusading endeavours (lasting well into the nineteenth century) to make Highlanders more like Lowlanders, the SSPCK relied principally on providing educational opportunities to young people – the Society eventually maintaining dozens of schools across the Highlands and Islands. And when, in the middle part of the eighteenth century, the SSPCK extended its activities into those parts of Britain's North American colonies still inhabited by Native Americans, much the same approach was adopted.

One of the many strengths of Margaret Connell Szasz's fascinating study is to be found in her realisation that both Highlanders and Native Americans adapted the learning that reached them from outside with a view to utilising this learning, and all that came with it, in ways which helped forge new identities more helpful than the old to people looking to safeguard at least something of their former ways of life while also coming to terms with the new social and cultural orders in which they found themselves. Szasz makes this point with particular reference to two individuals, Samson Occom, a Mohegan presbyterian preacher and teacher whom the SSPCK helped finance, and Dugald Buchanan, a Gaelic poet who served as one of the Society's schoolmasters and catechists – principally in the Rannoch district of Highland Perthshire. Szasz is intrigued, as I am, by the fact that, for a couple of months in 1767, Buchanan and Occom were simultaneously in Edinburgh, the former assisting with the translation of the New Testament into Gaelic, the latter raising funds needed to maintain and expand Christianising effort among the Algonquian tribes of New England. Whether Occom and Buchanan actually met is uncertain. But if they did, Margaret Szasz argues persuasively, they would have had much in common – both of them urging their people towards reformed protestantism but both of them also aiming, as Szasz puts it, 'to retain the cultural sovereignty of Algonquians and Highland Gaels'.

Native Americans who spent time in Scotland, as Samson Occom did, were few and far between. Traffic in the other direction was heavy; and, from the early eighteenth century forward, this traffic included growing numbers of Gaelic-speaking Highlanders. I have myself spent some time on the Flathead Indian Reservation in Montana with Indian people (their preferred term) who are descended from one such Highlander, a Hudson's Bay Company fur-trader, Angus McDonald, who also features in Colin G. Calloway's book. Had I then had access to Calloway's fine and comprehensive study, I would have had much less difficulty than in fact I experienced in writing meaningfully about the wider background into which I tried to fit the life and times of McDonald, his Nez Percé wife and their Métis (Calloway's preferred term) or mixed-blood sons and daughters. Calloway's book is, at one level, a valuable gathering together of what a whole series of historians and anthropologists have discovered about numerous Highlander-Native American relationships and connections of the Angus McDonald type. Beyond that, and still more valuably, his book – like Szasz's – demonstrates, to go back to where I started, that if we are ever properly to grasp how the Gaelic-speaking Highlands and Islands got from where they were in the fourteenth century to where they were 500 years later, we need to stop studying the Highlands and Islands in isolation. The region was not the special case it can easily seem when our focus is wholly on Scotland. What happened to Highland Gaels – whether the deliberate destruction of their kinship-based way of living or their subsequent romanticisation – happened also, although in more extreme and even less excusable ways, to Native Americans. And to be informed about both sets of experiences is to be better informed about each.

Neither Colin G. Calloway nor Margaret Connell Szasz are specialists in the history either of the Highlands and Islands or of Scotland more generally. Scottish historians, then, could readily go through their books, just as historians of Native Americans could go through my own account of Indian people called McDonald, with a view to finding dubieties of the sort that are unavoidable when anyone ventures beyond their own area of specialism. Perhaps it is because nit-picking of this sort appeals to many academics that excursions into comparative history are rarer than they ought to be. If so, given the quality of what is to be gained from those two excellent books, the nit-pickers need seeing off.

James Hunter
Centre for History, University of the Highlands and Islands

The Sutherland Estate, 1850–1920.
By Annie Tindley. Pp viii, 190.
ISBN 9780748640324 (hbk).
Edinburgh: Edinburgh University Press, 2010. £45.00.
DOI: 10.3366/nor.2011.0012

In the historiography of the highland clearances no name echoes with more persistent or negative resonance than that of the Sutherland family. Symbolising the generic dislocation and injustice of clearance policies across the highlands, the estate's notoriety was attributable to a combination of the scale and speed of reorganisation, the ideology that underpinned it and the ruthlessness with which it was executed, particularly by the notorious Patrick Sellar. Until now those traumatic events of the early nineteenth century have overshadowed the subsequent history of the largest landed estate in western Europe, despite the existence of a voluminous paper trail of estate records and other documentation covering a period that encompassed the crofters' war, ongoing land raiding and the genesis of crofting legislation, against the backdrop of the Sutherlands' declining territorial, political and social influence.

A superb antidote to that neglect has now been provided by Annie Tindley's forensically researched, carefully contextualised and immensely readable study. Its three central themes – the long-term legacy of the clearances, the changing philosophies and practices of estate management, and the Sutherlands' attempts to service their debts by radical territorial and financial restructuring – are put under the microscope in six substantive chapters, each of which not only distils and evaluates evidence from a wide range of sources, but also breathes life into many of the individuals who populate the archives. The Scourie factor Evander McIver, for instance – whose portrait graces the book's dust jacket – emerges as a reactionary old man rooted in the past, whose unwillingness to countenance changing economic and political conditions often put him at odds with the estate's upper management, the ducal family, and sometimes with his fellow factors.

Inter-managerial tensions are among the issues analysed in the first chapter, which addresses the estate management's fraught relations with its tenants during the 1850s and 1860s. The failure of clearance policies, particularly on the west coast, was reflected in intermittent crofter agitation, but while McIver wanted to take punitive action against those who engaged in 'illegal and violent conduct', the ducal family – as well as commissioners James and George Loch – were more concerned to prevent further damage to the estate's public image than to enforce discipline among crofters. They also contended with the radicalising influence of Free Church ministers, and – by 1870 – with the serious financial implications of the departure of the large sheep farming tenants whose rents had for long undergirded the estate's rent rolls.

The vast, but largely unknown land reclamation schemes implemented by George Loch and the third duke in an attempt to retain those sheep farmers and make the estate self-sufficient are the subject of chapter two. They were an expensive failure, in which an outlay of £210,870 generated a rent increase of only £800 per annum, although the duke managed to cloak the experiment with a patriotic gloss, presenting himself as a careful steward of his ancestral lands, a traditional clan leader and an astute businessman.

The collapse of the land reclamation schemes coincided with escalating crofter agitation throughout the highlands. Although direct action was rare on the Sutherland estate, the management's traditional perception of its small tenants as a social and economic burden was reinforced by the events of the 1880s. Much of chapter 3 is concerned with both sides' responses to the Napier Commission, responses that were shaped in different ways by the ghost of Patrick

Sellar. While crofters' complaints about insecure tenure, exorbitant rents, land hunger and uncompensated improvements echoed those of their counterparts across the region, they continued to blame their plight on 'tyrannical' factors rather than on the duke. He and his staff, meantime, were backed into a defensive corner by hostile press and public attention, but were disunited and ineffective in their reaction. Fault lines developed between factors and upper management, the former upholding the status quo in the face of demands by crofters who in the factors' view 'had never had it so good', but the latter realising that they could no longer act with impunity in ignoring or refusing tenants' petitions.

By 1886 these pressures had brought about a significant reorientation of estate management. During the ensuing decade – examined in chapter 4 – internal relations deteriorated further, as both crofters and management discovered that their experiences of the Crofters' Holdings Act failed to match expectations. R. M. Brereton, who had become commissioner in 1886, lasted only two years in post, losing out in the battle of wills with the veteran Evander McIver and the other factors. Resistance to his demand that they should uphold the spirit as well as the letter of crofting legislation was rooted in a fear – at least on McIver's part – that the Crofters' Commission would open the floodgates to rampant socialism among an 'ungrateful troublesome people' who were egged on by equally 'troublesome Clericals' to demand unfeasible land redistribution, particularly in the era of the Deer Forest Commission. Unstable management was exacerbated by the sudden death of the third duke in 1892 and the subsequent public wrangle over his frequently altered will. It was therefore little wonder, in these circumstances of administrative and financial upheaval, that the estate was unable to deal effectively with the fundamental reconfiguration of the highland socio-political order in the 1880s and 1890s.

Following McIver's retirement in 1895, the Sutherlands were able to bury some of the psychological legacies of famine and clearance. But the dawn of the twentieth century did not bring relief to either the estate management or its beleaguered tenants. Chapter 5 analyses the events of the early 1900s, when the Congested Districts Board made controversial – and ultimately unsuccessful – attempts to encourage land purchase by crofters until it was replaced by the Board of Agriculture for Scotland in 1911. The increasing intervention of government agencies in highland administration took place in Sutherland against the backdrop of sweeping territorial attrition, as land sales undertaken by the fourth and fifth dukes reduced the acreage of the estate from 1.1 million to 385,000 in twenty years. Also woven into the fabric of Sutherland life was the persistent non-payment of rents, which by that depressed period had become a consequence of 'poverty, rather than politics'.

The interaction of poverty, politics and personalities is demonstrated in the final substantive chapter, a longitudinal case study of an attempt to create a model farm in the clearance township of Clashmore in Assynt. The venture provoked a level of unrest unique to Sutherland, as well as an unusual degree of unity among the crofters in their opposition to the removals associated with the reclamation of 92 acres. The initial agitation of 1870–4 was renewed with greater intensity in 1884, when the expiry of the first tenant's lease led to unsuccessful crofter demands for their reinstatement on the land. The estate's refusal to compromise triggered rent strikes, deforcements and, in November 1887, following the transfer of the lease to the shipping magnate, David MacBrayne, the occupation of the farm and the destruction of its buildings by arson. The Clashmore controversy also highlighted once again the hard-line attitude of Evander McIver, resulting in the resignation of his bête-noire R. M. Brereton, after a major public disagreement over the latter's wish to make land grants to law-abiding crofters. In 1888, however, a degree of compromise was achieved through the intervention of the Crofters' Commission and in 1909 the entire farm was finally divided among 20 applicants.

Writing in 1898, Evander McIver delivered a disconsolate verdict on an enterprise that he had served for four decades but which had become a shadow of its former self. 'I am vexed and broken in spirit by the sale of so much of this fine estate that I cannot think, speak or write about it with patience' was his epitaph. The processes whereby the Sutherland estate lost its territorial, financial and political influence have been methodically charted in this important and easily-navigable study, which should be on the bookshelves not only of academics but also of readers with a general interest in the modern highlands.

There are many reasons that make it essential reading. Not least, it brings together a period of immense upheaval and political change in highland history and an estate with a combination of voluminous records, a highly contentious record of management and a controversial historiography. It is surprising that these general and specific themes have not been married before now. Written primarily from an estate-centric perspective, it scotches any concept of the Sutherland property as a well-oiled, integrated machine, highlighting instead the fractured, bureaucratic nature of estate management, and the persistent inter-managerial tensions that sometimes brought the administration to a virtual standstill. It embeds the Sutherland story in the wider, better-known historiography of late nineteenth- and early twentieth-century highland land reform, while simultaneously reflecting the long shadow cast by the estate's particular experience of the clearances. But, perhaps most importantly – and not least because of the judicious use of memorable quotes from the estate dinosaur, Evander McIver – it is a cracking good read!

Marjory Harper
University of Aberdeen

A History of Disability in Nineteenth-Century Scotland.
By Iain Hutchison. Pp. xi + 386.
ISBN 9780773452718 (hbk).
Lampeter: The Edwin Mellen Press, 2007. £79.95.
DOI: 10.3366/nor.2011.0013

In this interesting, thought-provoking and well written book, Iain Hutchison draws our attention to the significance of the place of people with disabilities in nineteenth-century Scotland. A central premise of the book is that the voice of people with disabilities has been missing from the way in which Scottish history has been constructed and that there is a need to listen carefully to these hidden voices. By gathering together a wide range of sources and perspectives Hutchison intends to give voice to a particularly oppressed group of people and in so doing, raise our consciousness not only to the historical implications of such voicing, but also for what that may tell us about the experience of disability today.

An original dimension of this book is the author's use of disability studies to help analyse historical experience. He assumes throughout that disability is not simply located in any particular physical or psychological impairment. Rather it is located in people's responses to the impairments they see in others. That being so, disability is a thoroughly social category that relates to the types of experiences that people with impairments had foisted upon them by Scottish society. Within Victorian Scotland 'disability' seems to have been primarily an economic category, being closely connected to a person's entitlement for relief under the Poor Law legislation. The Poor Law Act of 1845 in Scotland drew a distinction with regard to charitable relief between able-bodied and disabled people. Here a close tie between disability and lack of productivity emerged and was to some degree formalised: a tie that had implications for the perception and treatment of people with disabilities throughout Scotland. 'When disabled and able-bodied terminology was used, it was applied in terms of ability to work, and to entitlement or otherwise to poor relief or other forms of community support. Being disabled was not a direct reference to a physical, sensory or mental impairment, but to societal expectations of an individual being able to support him or herself and dependants.' (328)

The book begins by exploring the difficult issue of precisely how disability should be defined, before moving on to apply this analysis to the 'Othering' of people with disabilities, the ways in which they were portrayed in popular literature, the impact of this for life in community, in the institution, within society in general and for the types of personal relationships that were available. All of this with a specific focus on facilitating the voices of people with disabilities. The book is rigorous, engaging and filled with fascinating insights. For example, the observation that working-class communities were more sympathetic towards disability as they recognised that they were more likely to experience it raises quite sharply the ways in which economics, class and power combine both to define the nature and the consequences of disability, an insight that bears significant weight for modern-day Scotland. The use of narrative and experience makes it lively and yet poignant in its impact. Throughout the reader is introduced to interesting figures such as William Baillie who apparently lost his sanity whilst in Baghdad, the main reported symptoms of his condition being his conversion to Islam, and 'Daft Sandy' whose plea, 'I'm daft, man. Gies a bawbe', amused and perhaps frightened passengers travelling on public coaches in Dundee. The key point being that such voices are not secondary or illustrative: rather they are the primary sources that drive the book.

If there was a criticism it would be around the breadth of the definition of disability that underpins the study. Hutchison's holistic definition incorporates 'mental, physical and sensory disability, but also considers temporary as well as permanent disablement.' (29) This works well as a functional definition of disability insofar as it allows him to draw out the hidden economic dimensions of disablement. However, it sits less well with other aspects of disability studies. Ongoing arguments around whether or not disability and illness are the same thing are not discussed and the conflation of mental illness with learning disabilities under the banner of 'mental impairment' is problematic. But perhaps more importantly, if disability has not to do with physical or psychological function and has primarily to do with economics, then the boundaries of the category become difficult to discern. Presumably all poor people are disabled if they cannot work. Women are disabled if they cannot find employment or cannot work for whatever reason. Children are disabled until they are able to work and so forth. Such a broad and functional understanding of disability certainly makes the point and reframes disability in interesting ways. However, its breadth is both its strength and its weakness. Contemporary discussions around the minority group model of disability encounter similar problems. If the main thing that binds people with disabilities together is their status as a minority group rather than any particular shared impairment, then why would women, people of colour or people who are homosexual not be considered disabled alongside people with intellectual disabilities, mental illness, sight impairments or mobility issues? The problem is that disability is a difficult concept to tie down. Hutchison's work indicates that it was ever thus!

Overall the book works well in giving voice to people with disabilities and developing an economic basis for the development of the category of disability at that time. These are two important and easily overlooked observations that help to open up the broad range of experiences that people with disabilities went through during the period under investigation. The book should be welcomed and read by anyone who has a genuine interest in the history of disability and disability studies. It is a most worthy contribution to the field.

John Swinton
University of Aberdeen

Whaur Extremes Meet: Scotland's Twentieth Century.
By Catriona M. M. MacDonald. Pp. 427.
ISBN 9781906566081 (hbk).
Edinburgh: John Donald, 2009. £20.00.
DOI: 10.3366/nor.2011.0014

In November 2010 Catriona MacDonald's *Whaur Extremes Meet* won the prestigious Saltire Society History Book of the Year prize and it is wholly deserved. It is a hefty and rigorously researched book that tackles the complex and often painful realities of a nation caught in a perpetual struggle for stability, security and, ultimately, self-worth. The wonderfully human preface reminds us that this is a book about the lived experience of Scots in the twentieth century and that it would be a rough ride.

Her planning of this book is novel because it takes a thematic rather than a chronological approach and in choosing to write it this way, MacDonald allowed herself the freedom to engage with new historical dimensions. The book's thirteen chapters are arranged into four parts: In the Shadow of the Crane – Scotland's Economy; 'These Various Scotlands' – Scottish Society; 'The instinct for Freedom' – Twentieth-century Politics; and, finally, Cultural Extremes. A vein running through all parts is the relationship between the individual and the nation which, she convincingly argues, became more and not less complex as the century progressed. The acute tensions made manifest by unionism's increasing redundancy at the hands of global economic forces throw up new and perhaps more deliberate questions about what being Scottish actually means in today's world and whether or not it matters at all.

The four chapters that make up the first part, In the Shadow of the Crane – Scotland's Economy, spell out the disaster that became the manufacturing sector. The reluctance to let go of traditional industries and embrace innovation, entrepreneurship and the need for domestic investment sealed the fate of the industrial labourer. Even where new industries did emerge, the lack of any organic links with the old ones stifled potential for real growth and development. The economy was not able to diversify because there was a stubborn reluctance to let go of the belief that the public sector could and would save the Scottish economy. MacDonald points out that the debilitating attachment to the traditional industries meant that Scotland was ill-equipped to handle the international corporations that sought profit over sustainability. The banking and oil sectors, both of which had the potential to deliver significant benefits for the long-term growth of the Scottish economy, were governed by outside interests that had little regard for the needs of the nation.

Part Two, 'These Various Scotlands' – Scottish Society, considers themes including population, health and wellbeing, lifestyle, poverty, drugs, crime and the gender divide. It is an honest appraisal of a nation whose people were in trouble. In 1993, for example, MacDonald points out that one quarter of all Scots lived in poverty and that throughout the century plagues such as domestic violence and drug abuse wreaked havoc on society's most vulnerable. Women's ambitions were consistently curbed or restricted altogether and those who managed to move forward with education soon hit the impenetrable glass ceiling. The rise of youth crime should have alerted everyone that collective action was needed to give them something, anything to believe in but very little change was ever forthcoming. Importantly, MacDonald debunked the national myth that education in Scotland was egalitarian.

In the third part, 'The instinct for Freedom' – Twentieth-century Politics, the reader is provided with an excellent overview of local and national politics. MacDonald reveals how the decline of the independence of local office made Scotland more susceptible to the centralising power of Westminster. There is a very helpful overview of the Scottish Office, its changing responsibilities and the centralising quangos that were created to give the impression that the needs of Scotland were being met when in reality they merely enabled the Conservatives to influence Scottish politics. That the National Museums of Scotland was one such organisation might be something of a surprise for those unfamiliar with the demands of Scotland's mid-nineteenth-century pioneer unionist-nationalist organisation, the National Association for the Vindication of Scottish Rights. Finally, she provides an overview of the political parties, highlighting their rise and, in the case of the Liberals, their fall. Somewhat ironically, given the United Kingdom's current coalition government, she notes that 'there is nothing more logical and more doomed than a centre party'. The slow rise of nationalism towards the century's close was indicative of the union's inability to offer Scots what they felt they needed. No doubt this will be an area of considerable debate for some time to come.

The book's final part, Cultural Extremes, is a thought-provoking section that positions Scotland as a nation digging around in the trunks of its history to find something that would prove its distinctiveness and worth. The Scottish churches – all of them – demonstrated a resolve to fend off change and as a result of their inability to move with people as they sought new directions, cemented their own redundancy. Again, the desperation to hold on to tradition did Scotland few favours. The interesting discussion on art and literature demonstrates that whilst there was a willingness to engage with the dark side of life in Scotland, there was no real responsibility assumed by these industries to find solutions. Propped up by subsidies, the arts in Scotland were not as critical or successful as they could have been. They were often too insular and too inward-looking to be in a position to engage with the bigger picture that was developing around them. Sport, travel and the media should have given Scotland the opportunities to develop stronger relationships both within and beyond its borders but the same old story of outside control and internal division restricted their ability to accomplish this.

I read this book from the perspective of an educated outsider. I have studied this nation for the past ten years and have lived in it for a large part of that time and yet some of its characteristics still do not make sense to me. I struggle to understand the crippling lack of self-worth and confidence that plagues Scotland's youth and shapes generations. I understand, for example, the roots of sectarianism and the class divide though I cannot comprehend their continuance. I can see why emigration can be at once a source of intense pride and of deep pain and yet I do not know why the Irish, the Polish, the Jewish or the Asian immigrant, who has helped to build this nation, has never been allowed fully to belong to it. In attempting to provide an honest if uncomfortable and sometimes gloomy appraisal of a struggling nation, MacDonald has opened a number of windows and I feel like I know Scotland much better than I did. This is not just a great book because of the diligent and extensive research that went into to writing it, it is a great book because it has the potential to challenge people, historian and non-historian, academic and non-academic, to think more critically about this nation and its future.

This book is not for the faint hearted. It is a critical, unflattering, yet wholly necessary appraisal of a nation that has yet to understand itself and harness its potential because it does not yet know what its potential is. MacDonald does not write about the glory and greatness of Scotland – she engages directly and unashamedly with the internal and external problems it has faced on account of the inherent and debilitating tensions between tradition and modernity. There are many lessons to be learned from *Whaur Extremes Meet* and one can only hope that copies of this book find their way on to the desks of those politicians, policy shapers and business leaders who are brave enough to engage with the good, the bad and the ugly in twenty-first-century Scotland.

S. Karly Kehoe
Centre for History, University of the Highlands and Islands